# Table of Contents

# Part 1: Introduction to GPT-4 Chat

## 1.1 Understanding Artificial Intelligence and Language Models

### The Evolution of Language Models

Language models are at the forefront of AI research and represent a crucial component of many AI applications. In this chapter, we travel through time, examining the development of language models from their early beginnings to the present state-of-the-art advancements. We discuss key milestones, breakthroughs, and influential language models like GPT (Generative Pre-trained Transformer).

### Foundations of Natural Language Processing

To truly understand language models, one must grasp the fundamentals of Natural Language Processing (NLP). In this chapter, we provide an introduction to NLP, breaking down the intricacies of processing and analyzing human language. We explore techniques such as tokenization, stemming, lemmatization, and parsing that form the building blocks of language models.

**Neural Networks and Deep Learning**

Neural networks play a vital role in language modeling. In this chapter, we provide an overview of neural networks and deep learning, equipping readers with the knowledge required to comprehend the inner workings of language models. We discuss popular neural network architectures, such as recurrent neural networks (RNNs) and the transformative power of deep learning in shaping the AI landscape.

**Understanding the Mechanics of Language Models**

Now equipped with the necessary background, we dive into the mechanics of language models. This section explores the concepts of tokenization, attention mechanisms, and contextual embeddings, which enable language models to generate coherent and contextually relevant text. We also examine the training process, fine-tuning approaches, and evaluation of language models.

**Applications of Language Models**

In this chapter, we unveil the vast array of applications that utilize language models. We explore how language models power virtual assistants, translation services, chatbots, text generation, sentiment analysis, and information retrieval systems. Through real-world examples and case studies, we demonstrate the practical applications of language models in different domains.

**Ethical Considerations in AI and Language Models**

While AI and language models have incredible potential, they also raise important ethical considerations. In this chapter, we delve into ethical guidelines, biases in language models, privacy concerns, and the responsibility of AI developers in mitigating unintended consequences. Understanding the ethical implications is essential in ensuring the responsible and beneficial use of AI technology.

From understanding the foundations of AI to exploring the cutting-edge applications of language models, we hope to have provided you with a comprehensive introduction to this dynamic field. Remember, this is just the beginning of your exploration, and the possibilities are limitless.

**1.2 The Evolution of AI-Language Models: GPT-4 and Beyond**

Artificial intelligence (AI) is an ever-evolving field that continues to push the boundaries of human technological understanding. Over the years, researchers have strived to develop intelligent systems that can comprehend and even emulate human capabilities. One significant development in this domain is the advent of AI-language models.

These models are poised to revolutionize various industries such as natural language processing, conversation generation, personalized content creation, educational aids, and more. But before we delve into the state-of-the-art GPT-4 model and its successors, it is crucial to gain a clear understanding of the foundation on which they were built.

Starting from the early days when thin slivers of intelligent systems were developed, we will explore the progress in AI technologies that finally led to the creation of modern language models. Through insightful discussions, we will demystify complex subjects, making them easily graspable by beginners in this field.

Our exploration will trace the remarkable progress of language models like GPT (Generative Pre-trained Transformer), disclosed as GPT-1 by OpenAI, capturing every influential variant along the way. GPT-2 astounded the scientific community with its impressive capabilities for predicting and generating coherent text. Its multitudinous applications prompted a series of advancements and studies that laid the foundation for the higher-performing model, GPT-3.

Along the journey, we will analyze vast realms like unsupervised learning mechanisms, transfer learning processes, recursion, retrieval models, fine-tuning techniques, and training data biases that often caused significant ripples within the field. Each topic will provide a stepping stone in our understanding, ensuring that beginners grasp vital concepts en route to comprehending the progressively sophisticated GPT-4 model.

As GPT-4 emerges onto the scene, its novel components and state-of-the-art features introduce exciting developments accompanied by newfound challenges. Harnessing this model's remarkable power requires a nuanced understanding of its architecture, underpinning algorithms, training methods, and potential applications. We will dissect these intricate details, empowering readers to polish their AI-research prowess and explore experimental possibilities for future applications.

Moreover, as advancing technology poses crucial ethical implications, particularly concerning responsible AI development and fairness issues, we will extend our discussions to include vital considerations at each stage of the models' evolution. These discussions will promote an ethical mindset vital for developing AI models that align with moral and societal principles.

Enhanced by real-world examples, thoughtful anecdotes, and simplified case studies, this book endeavors to kindle the curiosity and interest of beginners exploring the world of AI-language models. By unraveling the complex evolution of GPT-4 and envisioning what lies beyond, readers will augment their foundational knowledge, inspiring further research, innovation, and responsible utilization in future AI systems.

It is my genuine hope that the readers will imbibe the intricacies of AI-language models, effectively fostering a precise understanding of GPT-4 and beyond to unlock the spectacular potential of this remarkable field. So, without further ado, let us delve into the enthralling tale of the AI-language models that continue to rewrite mans' encounter with machine intelligence.

**1.3 Benefits and Applications of GPT-4 Chat**

Human interaction is a fundamental aspect of our daily lives, enabling us to express thoughts, exchange knowledge, and foster connections with others. Over the years, there have been countless remarkable advancements in technology that have revolutionized the way we communicate. Among these breakthroughs is the development of sophisticated AI-powered chat platforms, capable of emulating intelligent conversational agents.

In today's technologically driven era, open dialogue with machines has become a reality thanks to the rapid progress in machine learning and natural language processing. These advancements have given rise to fascinating conversational AI models like GPT-4 Chat, which stands at the forefront of cutting-edge research and application in this area.

The introduction of GPT-4 Chat brings forth exciting possibilities, offering numerous benefits across several domains. This book sets out to explore the substantial advantages and the vast array of applications that GPT-4 Chat brings to the table, empowering creators, businesses, educators, and individuals worldwide.

One of the primary benefits of GPT-4 Chat lies in its ability to generate human-like responses by leveraging large-scale language models. This technology allows for more natural and engaging conversations, facilitating a genuine and interactive user experience. Through deep learning methods and extensive training on vast amounts of data, GPT-4 Chat demonstrates an impressive ability to understand context, learn from feedback, and adapt its response generation accordingly.

By utilizing GPT-4 Chat, content creators can harness the potential of AI-generated text to augment their creative process. Whether it be writing dialogue for video game characters, scripting movie scenes, generating content for social media platforms, bloggers, or publishers, GPT-4 Chat can lend a helping hand, offering suggestions and serving as a versatile tool through which new ideas can flourish.

Furthermore, GPT-4 Chat has immense potential in the world of e-commerce and customer service. Imagine a virtual assistant that can seamlessly handle customer inquiries, provide personalized product recommendations, and troubleshoot common issues, all while replicating human-like conversational interactions. With GPT-4 Chat, businesses can improve customer experiences, streamline operations, and reduce workload by employing AI-powered agents capable of comprehending and responding to user requests. The software garners the collective knowledge of an organization and alleviates the burden on support teams, allowing them to focus on pressing matters.

For educators, GPT-4 Chat represents a valuable instrument for disseminating knowledge and facilitating engaging learning experiences. Through intelligent tutoring systems, GPT-4 Chat can adapt to students' unique needs, offer personalized explanations, provide additional resources, and even act as a conversation partner for language learners. This technology supports the shifting landscape of education by delivering accessible and individualized instruction on a scale previously unimaginable.

While reaping the benefits of GPT-4 Chat, it is essential to navigate the associated ethical concerns and responsibilities as well. Neural networks can unintentionally perpetuate biases and produce potentially harmful content if not adequately designed and monitored. Promoting transparency, addressing bias, and implementing safeguards are crucial factors in its continued research and application.

GPT-4 Chat goes beyond examination as just a theoretical concept stemming from AI research labs — it is becoming an indispensable asset in various fields, thriving on its potential to simulate convincing and intelligent human-like interactions. Through this book, we delve into the transformative influence, endless possibilities, and ethical considerations surrounding GPT-4 Chat's unique ability to augment dialogues. By exploring its applications and benefits across sectors, we empower readers to embrace and utilize this extraordinary AI-powered technology in their everyday lives with confidence, curiosity, and responsibility.

## 1.4 Prerequisites: Basic Computer Skills and Familiarity with AI

Imagine a world where machines are not just able to perform a range of tasks, but also possess the capability to think, learn, and make informed decisions. This notion may seem like something out of a futuristic science fiction movie, but in reality, it is the realm of Artificial Intelligence (AI). AI has become one of the most exciting and rapidly evolving fields in the realm of technology, promising to revolutionize numerous industries and shape the way we live and work.

As an AI research expert, my aim in this book is to demystify the complex world of AI and make it accessible to beginners. While the topic of AI can be overwhelming, fear not! This book will serve as a stepping stone for anyone with a keen interest in AI who wants to build a solid foundation in this fascinating field.

Before we dive into the depths of AI, it is important to have a set of basic computer skills and a familiarity with the fundamentals of AI. In this chapter, we will discuss the prerequisites necessary to embark on this AI journey.

First and foremost, possessing basic computer skills is paramount. Familiarity with different operating systems, such as Windows, macOS, or

Linux, is essential. This includes knowing how to navigate through the file system, install and uninstall software applications, and perform basic computer operations like copying, pasting, and file management. Understanding how to use search engines effectively to find information is also crucial, as it will help you immensely throughout your AI learning process.

Furthermore, a basic understanding of programming concepts is highly advantageous. While not mandatory, learning a programming language, such as Python, will allow you to experiment with AI models and algorithms. Python, with its simplicity and vast support from AI libraries and frameworks, is widely regarded as the go-to language for AI beginners. Don't worry if you are new to programming; we will cover the necessary basics as we progress through this book.

Next, a basic understanding of mathematics and statistics is invaluable in grasping the underlying principles of AI algorithms. Concepts such as probability, linear algebra, and calculus are frequently used in AI applications. However, fear not if mathematics isn't your strong suit! I will explain these concepts in a beginner-friendly manner, making sure you comprehend the essentials without getting lost in intricate mathematical details.

Lastly, having a familiarity with the field of AI is advantageous. Understanding the broad categories of AI, such as machine learning, deep learning, and natural language processing, will provide you with a solid foundation to comprehend the intricacies of AI techniques. Becoming aware of real-world AI applications and the impact they have on various industries will spark your curiosity and drive to delve deeper into this field.

By obtaining and refining these prerequisites, you will find yourself well-prepared to embark on your AI journey. This chapter aims to ensure that you have the necessary groundwork laid out, allowing you to approach the upcoming topics with confidence and enthusiasm. So let's get started on this exciting adventure into the world of AI!

# Part 2: Setting Up GPT-4 Chat

**2.1 Obtaining Access to GPT-4**

In recent years, artificial intelligence (AI) has experienced remarkable advancements. Among these, one of the most fascinating achievements has been the development of Generative Pre-trained Transformers (GPTs). These powerful models have revolutionized various fields by demonstrating unprecedented abilities in natural language processing and generation. GPT-4, the fourth iteration of the GPT series, is the pinnacle of this technological evolution and marks the cutting edge in language generation.

However, gaining access to such advanced AI models may initially seem daunting, especially for beginners. This chapter aims to alleviate any concerns or confusion surrounding the process of obtaining access to GPT-4. Whether you are an AI enthusiast, a student, or a professional seeking to leverage the potential of GPT-4, this comprehensive guide will equip you with the necessary knowledge and steps to navigate the journey effectively.

**Understanding GPT-4:**

Before delving into the details of accessing GPT-4, it is crucial to develop a holistic understanding of this impressive AI model. GPT-4 is a large-scale deep learning model that operates on the principles of unsupervised learning. It is pre-trained on vast amounts of text data from the internet, enabling it to capture intricate linguistic patterns, semantics, and contextual information. This implicit knowledge empowers GPT-4 to generate coherent and contextually relevant responses to prompts or queries.

GPT-4 boasts a significantly enhanced architecture compared to its predecessors, resulting in improved performance, a larger parameter size, and increased capabilities in understanding and generating text. Its training process involves complex techniques, leveraging state-of-the-art methodologies like unsupervised learning, attention mechanisms, and transformer networks. Understanding these underlying concepts will aid your comprehension of the subsequent sections discussing access acquisition.

**Access Channels:**
Securing access to GPT-4 involves contacting the organization responsible for its development and

deployment. While the exact channels for obtaining access may vary from organization to organization, there are some common avenues to explore:

**Academic Collaborations:**
Many organizations offer collaborations or partnerships with academic institutions. This collaboration allows researchers and students to gain access to cutting-edge AI models, including GPT-4. Academic collaborations often involve a formal application process, and if approved, researchers can gain access to specific resources, documentation, and sometimes even restricted APIs.

**Research Grants and Scholarships:**
Certain organizations may provide research grants or scholarships designed to support AI research endeavors. These grants can provide funding and access to resources, including access to advanced AI models like GPT-4. Exploring opportunities for research grants or scholarships can be a fruitful avenue for securing access to GPT-4.

**Commercial Licensing or Subscription:**

In some cases, organizations may offer commercial licensing or subscription models for accessing their AI models. These arrangements often cater to enterprises or individuals seeking to harness the capabilities of GPT-4 for commercial purposes. Commercial licensing typically involves contract negotiations, fees, and intellectual property considerations.

**Open-Source Alternatives:**
While GPT-4 itself may not be available as open-source, there might be variations or similar models developed and released by the AI community. Leveraging open-source alternatives can be an option for those who cannot directly access GPT-4 but still seek to explore and contribute to the field. These open-source models provide a platform for experimentation and research.

Access to GPT-4, with its exceptional natural language processing and generation capabilities, opens up a realm of possibilities for various domains. While obtaining access may require navigating specific channels, such as academic collaborations, research grants, commercial licensing, or open-source alternatives, the benefits of harnessing GPT-4's power make the endeavor worthwhile.

The subsequent sections will delve deeper into each access channel, guiding you through the steps and considerations involved. By the end of this book, you will have gained the knowledge and insights necessary to pave your way towards accessing and utilizing GPT-4 effectively, empowering you to embark on a transformative AI journey.

## 2.2 Installation and Configuration of GPT-4 Chat
### Understanding GPT-4 Chat

To set the stage for our exploration, we will start by providing a comprehensive overview of GPT-4 Chat. We will explain the underlying architecture and the mechanisms that enable it to generate remarkably human-like responses. Additionally, we will elaborate on the capabilities of GPT-4 Chat, its strengths, limitations, and potential applications across various sectors such as customer service, education, and entertainment.

### System Requirements

Installing and configuring GPT-4 Chat requires a thorough understanding of the computer infrastructure needed to support this high-performance model. In this chapter, we will outline the system requirements that must be met to fully utilize its capabilities. We will cover the necessary hardware specifications, software dependencies, and provide guidance on optimizing system performance.

**Obtaining GPT-4 Chat**

Before we dive into the installation process, we need to acquire the GPT-4 Chat software itself. In this chapter, we will guide you through the process of obtaining this state-of-the-art AI model. We will discuss different licensing options, availability, and explore the resources provided by the model developers for implementation support.

**Installation Process**

In this information-rich chapter, we will walk you through the step-by-step process of installing GPT-4 Chat. We will cover everything from setting up the necessary software dependencies, downloading the model files, and configuring your development environment. Clear instructions will be provided regardless of your operating system, ensuring a smooth installation experience.

**Configuration Options**

GPT-4 Chat is designed to be highly customizable, allowing users to define chat behavior, tailor responses, and customize the model's characteristics to meet specific requirements. In this chapter, we will explain the various configuration options available and guide you through the process of fine-tuning the model. We will discuss parameters like temperature, top-k and top-p sampling techniques, and offer best practices to achieve optimal results.

**Training and Data Considerations**

To enhance the performance of GPT-4 Chat in particular contexts or domains, it may be necessary to train the model with specific datasets. In this chapter, we will familiarize you with the methodologies and considerations involved in training the model on your custom data. We will discuss data collection, data preprocessing techniques, and strategies for avoiding biases in the trained model.

**Deploying GPT-4 Chat**

In the final stages of our journey, we will shine a light on the deployment process of GPT-4 Chat, ensuring seamless integration with your application or platform. This chapter will take you through the steps necessary to deploy the chatbot efficiently and securely. We will touch upon aspects such as scalability, load balancing, API management, and provide insights into potential challenges that may arise during deployment.

As AI continues to revolutionize the way we interact with technology, GPT-4 Chat stands at the forefront of conversational AI models, offering unprecedented abilities in natural language processing and generation. By following the detailed instructions and advice provided in this book, beginners will have a solid understanding of how to install and configure GPT-4 Chat, granting them the knowledge to harness the true potential of this extraordinary AI model. We hope this book serves as an invaluable resource in your journey to master the realm of GPT-4 Chat and create conversational AI experiences that push the boundaries of what humans thought possible.

## 2.3 Exploring the GPT-4 Chat User Interface

GPT-4, an advanced language model developed by OpenAI, is gaining immense popularity for its ability to generate human-like text. With its unique feature of contextual understanding and conversational capability, GPT-4 has revolutionized the field of artificial intelligence.

In this comprehensive guide, we delve deep into GPT-4's chat user interface, thoroughly exploring its functions, features, and applications for beginners like you. Whether you are an AI enthusiast, a language model researcher, or a developer intrigued by GPT-4, this book is designed to provide you with the knowledge and skills to interact effectively with this powerful chat system.

We begin our exploration by presenting an overview of the GPT-4 chat user interface and gradually progress towards explaining its essential components. You will gain insights into the architectural design of GPT-4 and understand how it performs in dialog-based tasks. We don't assume any prior knowledge or technical expertise, ensuring that beginners find this book informative and easy to understand.

As we uncover the inner workings of GPT-4, you will become familiar with the process of generating responses. We discuss the pre-training and fine-tuning stages that shape the model's ability to provide coherent and contextually relevant answers in a chat-based format. Moreover, we dive into the innovative techniques employed by OpenAI to enhance GPT-4's capabilities and address common challenges associated with language models.

Further, we explore the customization options offered by OpenAI, enabling developers to tailor the behavior of the GPT-4 chat interface more effectively. We shed light on the topic of fine-tuning and outline the steps to fine-tune the model on your specific use case or domain. This customization feature allows you to harness the power of GPT-4 to handle industry-specific queries, provide customer support, curate content, and bolster various other applications.

Integrating GPT-4 into your projects constitutes an exciting aspect of our discussion. We guide you through the process of utilizing OpenAI's powerful API to interact with GPT-4 and unleash its potential across different domains. Detailed examples and code snippets complement our explanations, allowing you to derive practical benefits from your association with GPT-4's chat user interface.

However, it's not solely about exploring GPT-4; we endeavor to address ethical considerations to ensure responsible usage of this technology. Reliability, privacy implications, bias, and security concerns are some of the key factors we touch upon, ensuring you employ GPT-4 in a manner that fosters transparency and builds trust with your users.

Additionally, while understanding a technology like GPT-4 is important, gaining practical exposure is equally advantageous. As part of this book, we incorporate interactive exercises and challenges that prudently reinforce your comprehension and strengthen your skills in using GPT-4.

Finally, we emphasize real-world applications and share inspiring success stories from professionals and organizations who have benefited immensely from integrating GPT-4 into their workflows. These case studies will captivate your imagination and motivate you to explore new frontiers with the transformative power of GPT-4, pushing the boundaries of what's possible with this cutting-edge technology.

With our comprehensive approach, clear and concise explanations, and hands-on exercises, this book equips aspiring AI enthusiasts, researchers, and developers with the knowledge needed to make the most out of GPT-4's chat user interface. By the end, you will have a solid understanding of GPT-4's capabilities, unmatched conversational ability, and its potential to redefine the way machines comprehend and generate language.

# Part 3: Navigating the GPT-4 Chat Interface

### 3.1 Understanding the Structure of Conversations

Conversations are an essential aspect of human interaction, enabling individuals to exchange information, share ideas, and establish meaningful connections with one another. From casual chit-chats to formal debates, conversations play a pivotal role in our daily lives.

Understanding the structure of conversations is crucial as it allows us to decipher the underlying patterns, rules, and dynamics that govern effective communication. By unraveling these intricate structures, we can navigate conversations with greater confidence and fluency, leading to more successful and productive exchanges.

To comprehend the structure of conversations, we need to delve into its fundamental components. We will explore how conversations typically begin with an opening, where participants introduce themselves and set the tone for the interaction. Openings often involve greetings, pleasantries, or other forms of small talk that help establish rapport and create a comfortable atmosphere.

As conversations progress, they evolve through various phases, each serving a specific purpose. One such phase is the information exchange stage, where participants share facts, opinions, and experiences. This phase requires active listening, as individuals must process and respond to the information being presented. It is essential to grasp the importance of turn-taking during this stage, ensuring that all participants have an opportunity to contribute their thoughts and ideas.

Another crucial phase is the negotiation stage, where participants engage in a dialogue to discuss differing viewpoints, negotiate agreements, or reach a consensus. This stage often involves the use of persuasive techniques, argumentation, and compromise. Understanding the underlying structure of negotiation can empower individuals to express their opinions effectively and achieve desired outcomes.

Finally, conversations conclude with a closing, which provides an opportunity to summarize key points, express gratitude, and politely end the interaction. Closings are essential in leaving a lasting impression and maintaining positive relationships.

Throughout this chapter, we will explore various conversational structures, including dyadic conversations (between two individuals), group discussions, interviews, and more. By analyzing and understanding these different structures, beginners can develop the skills necessary to engage in effective and meaningful conversations across diverse contexts.

Moreover, we will delve into the importance of non-verbal cues and gestures in understanding conversation structure. Body language, facial expressions, and tone of voice can convey hidden meanings that complement or even contradict verbal communication. Recognizing and interpreting these non-verbal elements is essential for comprehending the true nature of conversations.

Mastering the structure of conversations is a fundamental skill for effective communication. By understanding the different phases, turn-taking, negotiation, and the role of non-verbal cues, beginners can navigate conversations with confidence and proficiency. Through practice, observation, and thoughtful analysis of conversation structures, individuals can enhance their communication skills and become skilled conversationalists.

## 3.2 Initiating Conversations with GPT-4

**Initiating Conversations with GPT-4**
We will delve into the fascinating world of initiating conversations with GPT-4, the latest iteration of Generative Pre-trained Transformer technology. GPT-4 represents a significant milestone in the development of Conversational AI, bringing us closer to achieving more engaging and human-like interactions. This chapter will equip beginners with the necessary knowledge and techniques to effectively initiate conversations with GPT-4, enabling them to harness its immense potential.

Understanding the Role of GPT-4 in Conversations:
Before exploring the methods to initiate conversations with GPT-4, it is crucial to grasp

the role this AI model plays in conversational interactions. GPT-4 is designed to generate responses based on the context provided to it. It does not possess real-time awareness of the world or access to external knowledge; instead, it relies on pre-existing information within its training data. This distinction is essential to remember as you begin conversing with GPT-4.

**Setting Context:**
To elicit coherent and relevant responses from GPT-4, it is imperative to set a clear and concise context at the beginning of a conversation. Contextual information helps GPT-4 understand and interpret subsequent prompts effectively. This context can include relevant background details, past interactions, or any other relevant information that helps GPT-4 better comprehend the direction of the conversation.

**Initial Prompt Strategies:**
Crafting an effective initial prompt is crucial to initiate conversations with GPT-4. Consider the following strategies to achieve optimal results:

   a. Specificity: Being specific in your initial prompt can provide GPT-4 with a well-defined starting point. This helps guide the conversation and ensures the generated response aligns with your intended direction.

b. Clear Questions: Asking direct questions is an effective way to engage GPT-4 and obtain specific answers. By structuring your prompt as a question, you encourage GPT-4 to formulate a response that aligns with the query.

c. Context Inclusion: Reminding GPT-4 about relevant information from prior interactions or supplying necessary data points can serve as an anchor for generating responses. By explicitly referencing the context within the prompt, you facilitate a more focused and coherent conversation.

**Handling Incomplete or Insufficient Prompts:**
In some instances, you may find the initial prompt vague, incomplete, or lacking sufficient details. To address this, consider incorporating the following practices:

a. Paraphrasing: If the prompt is ambiguous, try paraphrasing or rephrasing it to provide additional clarity. This helps GPT-4 understand your intentions more accurately and generates responses aligned with your expectations.

b. Expanding Prompts: In scenarios where the prompt lacks vital details, it is advisable to expand on the information provided. By elaborating on essential aspects, you provide GPT-4 with more material to generate informative and relevant responses.

c. Iterative Feedback: If GPT-4's initial response does not align with your expectations, consider providing explicit feedback. Iteratively refining and specifying your prompt based on the generated responses can steer the conversation in the desired direction.

**Experimenting with Different Prompts:**
Conversational AI is an evolving field, and as a beginner, it is essential to experiment with various prompt styles and structures. By exploring different approaches, you can gain insights into how GPT-4 interprets and responds to different types of inputs. This hands-on experimentation will enhance your proficiency and enable you to elicit more accurate and contextually appropriate responses.

Initiating conversations with GPT-4 marks the beginning of exploring the world of

Conversational AI. By understanding the role of GPT-4, employing effective prompt strategies, and adapting to incomplete prompts, beginners can unlock the immense potential of this AI model. Remember to experiment and iterate, as becoming proficient in conversational interactions with GPT-4 entails continuous learning and refinement.

In a conversational AI system, the ability to maintain and manage effective context throughout a conversation is crucial for providing a seamless and personalized user experience. Imagine engaging in a chat with a virtual assistant, asking a series of questions or making requests. It would be frustrating if the system forgot the context of your conversation and constantly required you to repeat information. Effective context management tackles this challenge by enabling the system to remember and utilize past interactions to infer user intent accurately.

This section of the book delves into various techniques and strategies that empower developers to build conversational AI systems capable of managing and utilizing conversation context efficiently. We will discover how context can be preserved, handled, and employed to enhance linguistic flexibility and understand users' needs in a continuous conversation.

To comprehend the significance of conversational context management in AI systems, one must first understand the concept of context itself. Context encompasses the entire history of the conversation, including information provided, user queries, and system responses, allowing for a dynamically changing environment. It includes not only the immediate dialog but also the broader context like user preferences, session history, and task-related information. Effectively maintaining this context allows the system to exhibit intelligence by interpreting user inputs and delivering appropriate responses while adapting to the user's evolving needs.

Within this chapter, we will explore various core components essential for managing conversational context effectively.

### 3.3 Managing Conversational Context
**User Memory:**
User memory acts as a crucial component of context management by enabling the system to remember relevant user-specific information

during a conversation. This entails remembering preferences, personal details, preferences, demographic information, or any previous user inputs to develop a comprehensive understanding of the user's background.

**Conversation Memory:**
In addition to user memory, conversation memory plays a vital role in continuous context management. Contextual history needs to be stored throughout a conversation as this information becomes relevant during subsequent interactions. Lack of perspective can disrupt meaningful and coherent conversations. Memory allows an AI system to understand references to previous interactions and gather crucial information implicitly, making the system more natural and adaptive.

**Entity Tracking:**
Correctly identifying and tracking entities being discussed throughout a conversation is pivotal for managing conversational context. Entities are relevant keywords or information that aids in understanding user intents. Utilizing entity tracking, AI systems can accurately retain pertinent details throughout conversations,

eliminating the need for users to repeatedly provide information already mentioned.

**Coreference Resolution:**
An essential ability within conversational AI context management is coreference resolution. It involves accurately identifying pronouns or other expressions referring to a previous context and associating them correctly while generating a response. By resolving coreferences correctly, system responses become more coherent and maintain continuity within the conversation.

Throughout this chapter, we will provide detailed explanations, examples, and practical tips for implementing effective context management within your conversational AI systems. Rich context management ensures a user-friendly experience by reducing redundancy, aiding comprehension, offering natural responses, and recalling crucial information across conversations.

With a solid understanding of the principles and techniques behind managing conversational context, developers can create more sophisticated AI systems that comprehensively interpret users' needs and intent. By employing the concepts explored in this chapter, you will be well-equipped to enhance the context management capabilities of your conversational AI applications. So let's dive in and explore the intricacies of managing conversational context to level up your AI building skills!

**3.4 Utilizing System-Level Instructions**
In the world of Artificial Intelligence (AI), achieving optimal performance and efficiency is a constant pursuit. The growing demands for faster and more powerful AI systems have led to the development of specialized hardware and advanced techniques to maximize the utilization of available resources. One of the key areas where developers can enhance their AI applications is by harnessing the power of system-level instructions.

System-level instructions, also known as "primitives", refer to low-level commands or operations that are directly supported by the underlying hardware architecture. These instructions offer developers a way to efficiently utilize the resources provided by the system, such as the central processing unit (CPU) or graphics processing unit (GPU). By understanding and strategically employing system-level instructions, developers can significantly speed up computations and optimize their AI algorithms.

In this chapter, we delve into the realm of system-level instructions and explore their significance in AI programming. We aim to provide beginners with a comprehensive understanding of how these instructions can be utilized to enhance the performance of AI models and applications.

To embark on this journey, we first lay the foundation by introducing the concept of system-level instructions and their role in AI programming. We explain how different hardware architectures, such as CPUs and GPUs, have their own unique set of instructions and capabilities. By grasping these fundamentals, readers will gain insights into the underlying mechanisms that empower AI systems to deliver remarkable results.

Next, we delve deeper into the practical aspects of utilizing system-level instructions. We unravel the techniques to identify and exploit the available instructions, as well as explore various programming languages and frameworks that support system-level instruction utilization. Furthermore, we discuss the advantages and challenges associated with utilizing these instructions, enabling readers to make informed decisions while designing and optimizing their AI systems.

Moreover, we emphasize the importance of optimizing AI systems for different hardware platforms. As AI applications are often deployed on diverse devices ranging from personal computers to edge devices and cloud servers, understanding the hardware-specific instructions becomes essential. We explore how developers can adapt their algorithms and utilize the appropriate system-level instructions to achieve the best possible performance across different platforms.

In addition to the theoretical aspects, this chapter also provides practical examples and case studies to illustrate the real-world impact of utilizing system-level instructions. We showcase scenarios where the use of these instructions has led to significant speedups and increased efficiency in various AI applications, including image and speech recognition, natural language processing, and robotics.

By the end of this chapter, beginners in AI programming will have a solid grasp of the importance of system-level instructions and how to leverage them to unlock the full potential of AI systems. Armed with this knowledge, readers will be able to optimize their AI algorithms, boost computation speeds, and ultimately build cutting-edge AI applications that deliver exceptional performance.

So, let us embark on this enlightening journey through the realm of system-level instructions and witness the transformational impact they can have on AI programming.

# Part 4: Customizing GPT-4 Chat

**4.1 Incorporating User Personality and Context**

As AI systems continue to develop and evolve, their ability to understand and cater to the diverse needs, inclinations, and personalities of individual users will play a vital role in their efficacy and acceptance. To address this challenge, researchers have focused their attention on infusing user personality and context into AI systems, thus creating an enhanced sense of connection and engagement.

User personality refers to the unique traits, preferences, and characteristics that define an individual and influence their behavior and decision-making. It encompasses various aspects, such as interests, values, attitudes, and emotional dispositions. Context, on the other hand, portrays the broader setting in which interactions occur – it incorporates environmental elements, previous interactions, user history, and other situational factors that significantly influence user behavior and expectations at any given moment.

Understanding user personality and context profoundly impacts the success of AI system outputs, making them feel more human-centric, empathetic, and adaptive. By taking these factors into account, integrated AI systems can gracefully curate and deliver personalized recommendations, communicate in a manner aligned with the user's disposition, and intelligently adapt to different contextual signals.

Considering user personality involves analyzing data related to user behavior, interactions, and preferences. Leveraging psychological theories and models, AI systems can make accurate predictions about a user's individual traits. For example, a personality analysis can ensure that an AI recommendation engine tailors Netflix movie suggestions by considering the user's interests, resulting in a more satisfactory personalized viewing experience.

Contextual factors provide critical information about the immediate situation in which AI systems are deployed. These include circumstances, setting, time, location, and other variables that affect the interaction. Such information can empower an AI assistant to offer more intent-specific responses. For instance, when you pose a question to a voice-activated device about the nearby restaurants, it should provide the most relevant information that depends on factors like your physical location, the time of day, and your dietary preferences.

Designing AI systems to intuitively incorporate user personality and context entails several challenges. Principles of ethics, privacy, and user consent must be honored throughout the process. Aggregating user data while preserving privacy safeguards remains an intricate task for AI engineering teams, requiring rigorous data protection measures and secure storage approaches.

Building individual AI models embedded with user personality and context can significantly raise deployment complexity. Ensuring scalability while training models large enough to include the massive variations encountered in users' personalities and real-life situations requires ample computational resources and robust architectural designs.

Understanding and utilizing specialized algorithms for smartly exploiting user personality and context are vital steps toward evoking pleasurable, richer user experiences. Implementations leveraging machine learning techniques, such as reinforcement learning and natural language processing, can further compartmentalize user traits and preferences to generate articulate responses. Phenomena like transfer learning can enable AI systems to transfer knowledge about one user's personality to personalize interactions with another user.

By effectively incorporating user personality and context within AI systems, the doors to vast improvements in personalization and customization open. From recommender systems to educational platforms and many other domains, understanding user behavior and needs at a deeper level allows technology to operate as an insightful and invaluable personal assistant. The contributions made through meticulous research efforts in this field continue to crown our modern AI landscape with unmatched intelligence and engender remarkable human-like experiences while interacting with machines.

## 4.2 Fine-tuning GPT-4 for Specific Use Cases

Explore the concept and process of fine-tuning OpenAI's GPT-4 language model to better suit specific use cases. Fine-tuning provides a powerful tool for adapting pretrained models to a wide range of domains and applications, resulting in enhanced performance and more effective utilization of the underlying AI capabilities.

Before delving into the details, it is essential to grasp the fundamental idea behind the fine-tuning process. Large-scale language models, such as GPT-4, are pre-trained on vast amounts of data containing diverse sources and expertise. This pre-training imparts the models with a broad understanding of human language, grammar, syntax, and contextual relationships.

However, this general-purpose understanding may not directly align with the specific requirements and nuances of individual domains or tasks. Fine-tuning enables us to bridge this gap by tailoring the pre-trained model to meaningful applications such as medical data analysis, customer support interactions, legal document review, or any other targeted area.

Let's explore the different steps involved in the process of fine-tuning. But before we proceed, ensure that you have a good understanding of the foundational concepts explained earlier in this book.

**Define the Task:** Prior to initiating fine-tuning, clearly delineate the specific task or use case you want GPT-4 to perform better on. It could be generating coherent scientific papers, resolving customer billing complaints, responding accurately to medical queries, or generating creative solutions to a particular problem.

**Dataset Creation:** The effectiveness of fine-tuning relies heavily on having apt and well-annotated examples of input-output pairs that reflect the desired outcome for the specific task. Constructing an appropriate dataset involves carefully curating and generating data that is representative of the particular problem you aim to address. Depending on your specific needs, labels and annotations play a significant role in generating desired outputs.

**Model Configuration:** Once you have appropriately defined the task and set up the dataset, it's time to prepare the GPT-4 model for fine-tuning. Decisions regarding model size, parameter tuning, and hyperparameters need to be made. Fine-tuning offers flexibility here — you can choose to keep GPT-4 model's underlying architecture intact or modify it, if necessary, to align better with your specific needs. Finding the balance requires an understanding of the trade-offs involved and being mindful of not losing what has already been learned during pre-training.

**Training Process:** Training the fine-tuned model follows a similar process to pre-training but with a key change. Instead of the Broad Web Corpus adopted in pre-training, tasks specific to your domain are included. Finely adjusting the model on the targeted dataset lets the model consolidate its knowledge and approaches newer problem categories swiftly. Naturally, the availability of computing resources and time required will depend on the complexity and scale of your undertaking.

**Evaluation and Iterative Refinement:** Evaluating model performance is crucial for meaningful results. This assessment might include metric calculations and, where suitable, human review. Just like any iterative learning process, you may identify imperfections or inconsistencies that must be remedied. Extra iterations involving dataset revision, model tweaking, and fine-tuning might be necessitated to achieve the desired outcome.

Fine-tuning GPT-4 for specific use cases holds immense potential for numerous enterprises, researchers, and practitioners. The advent of fine-tuned models with accurate domain adaptation can revolutionize application-based outcomes. Utilizing targeted customization allows us to maximize the value and capability of even the most widespread and generalized AI frameworks.

**4.3 Creating Custom Prompts for Improved Responses**
Delve into the fascinating realm of creating custom prompts to enhance the responsiveness of AI models. Custom prompts offer a unique opportunity to tailor the behavior and output of AI systems according to our specific requirements and desired results.

Developing AI models with predefined tasks and query formulations allows us to generate highly targeted responses. However, these predefined setups may sometimes fall short in displaying the desired level of comprehension or accommodating unusual or nuanced queries. This is where the power of custom prompts comes into play, enabling us to fine-tune AI responses to match our needs more effectively.

The process of creating custom prompts involves framing questions, statements, or instructions in a carefully designed manner to guide the AI model towards more desirable outputs. By experimenting with various prompt structures, formats, and complexities, we can steer the model towards generating coherent and reliable responses that align with our goals.

Constructing custom prompts requires an understanding of how AI systems interpret commands and queries, as well as knowledge about the underlying tasks they are designed to fulfill. We need to be mindful of the underlying intent within our prompt and ensure that it caters to the specific requirements of the AI model we are working with.

In this chapter, we will explore the fundamental concepts and techniques involved in crafting effective custom prompts. We will examine how to design prompts that encourage fruitful exploration of complex topics and yield insightful responses, rather than generating misleading or uninformative outputs. Additionally, we will discuss strategies to prompt the model with context-rich inputs to improve the coherence and relevance of its replies.

Moreover, we will learn about optimizing prompts for different AI models and tasks. From fine-tuning language models to generating more creative or factual answers, to shaping the behavior of AI models to follow certain ethical guidelines, custom prompts offer us a versatile toolbox to mold AI systems according to our specific needs.

Throughout the chapter, we will illustrate our discussions with real-world examples and practical exercises. These examples will highlight the challenges associated with choosing the right prompts and showcase the impact that well-crafted prompts can have on the quality of AI-generated responses. By following the provided guidelines and undertaking the exercises, readers will acquire essential skills and knowledge needed to excel at crafting custom prompts for optimizing AI model outputs.

It is important to stress that custom prompts must be employed responsibly and ethically. As AI interacts more intimately with human knowledge and understanding, it becomes necessary for prompt designers to tackle issues related to biases, adversarial stimuli, cultural sensitivity, and inclusivity. This chapter will address these concerns and offer guidelines to create prompts that align with values of fairness, accuracy, and respect.

The art and science of creating custom prompts hold immense potential for refining AI outputs. With careful consideration, experimentation, and a strong grasp of underlying concepts, anyone can harness the power of custom prompts to obtain more accurate and tailored responses from AI models. By the end of this chapter, readers will be equipped with the knowledge and tools necessary to wield this technique effectively, empowering them to explore diverse fields, tackle challenges, and unlock the true potential of AI.

## 4.4 Adjusting Model Behavior through Parameters

Explored the fundamental concepts of artificial intelligence and the various techniques used in building models. We have discussed the importance of selecting an appropriate algorithm and understanding its core workings to ensure effective performance. However, as any AI practitioner will attest, the outcome of a model is not solely determined by the selected algorithm; it is also greatly influenced by the parameters chosen during the training and inference processes. This crucial aspect of adjusting model behavior through parameters is the focus of this section.

When constructing an AI model, the process typically involves specifying a set of parameters that influence its behavior. Parameters, in this context, are the variables that define the model's characteristics and shape its ability to analyze and understand the given data. These parameters essentially act as dials that can be turned to enhance or fine-tune the model's performance.

One important concept related to parameters is their initial values. Before training a model, parameters are generally initialized to specific starting values. The selection of initial values plays a crucial role as it can impact the model's convergence during the training process. Poorly chosen initial values may lead to models getting stuck in suboptimal solutions or being unable to learn effectively. Therefore, understanding how to appropriately initialize parameters is vital for achieving optimal performance.

Additionally, during the training process, parameters are adjusted by employing various optimization techniques. These techniques aim to iteratively update the parameters in a way that minimizes the error or loss function of the model. The specific optimization algorithms utilized, such as gradient descent or stochastic gradient descent, determine the pace and direction of parameter updates. Decisions made regarding the optimization algorithm can significantly impact a model's convergence, training duration, and overall accuracy.

While adjusting model behavior through parameters primarily refers to the training phase, parameters also play a vital role during the inference or prediction phase. In some cases, altering certain parameters can lead to improved model performance during inference. For example, adjusting the decision threshold in a binary classification model can help prioritize precision over recall or vice versa, depending on the specific use case.

Additionally, determining the optimal values for parameters can be a challenging task. It often involves employing strategies such as grid search or random search to iterate through different parameter settings and evaluate their impact on model performance. This process can be time-consuming and computationally intensive, highlighting the importance of efficient parameter tuning techniques.

Understanding the mechanisms by which parameters influence model behavior empowers AI practitioners to optimize and fine-tune their models effectively. It enables them to strike a balance between accuracy and generalization, ensuring that the model can capture patterns in the given data while avoiding overfitting or underfitting. Moreover, the ability to adjust model behavior through parameter manipulation plays a crucial role in addressing specific requirements and constraints of diverse real-world applications.

We will delve into the practical aspects of adjusting model behavior through parameters. We will explore strategies for parameter initialization, optimization algorithms, and techniques for efficient parameter tuning. By gaining a comprehensive understanding of these concepts, you will be equipped with the tools needed to optimize your AI models and enhance their performance to tackle real-world challenges effectively.

# Part 5: Advanced GPT-4 Chat Techniques

### 5.1 Utilizing Tokens and Tokenization

Delve into the fascinating world of Natural Language Processing (NLP). NLP is a branch of artificial intelligence that focuses on teaching computers to understand and process human language in a way that resembles human understanding. It provides the foundation for many of the applications we use daily, such as voice assistants, machine translation, sentiment analysis, and search engines.

As we progress through this book, we aim to equip beginners with a comprehensive understanding of NLP, starting from the fundamentals and gradually building up to more advanced topics. Our goal is to provide readers with the necessary knowledge and tools to embark on their own exciting NLP projects.

So, let us now explore Section 5.1, where we will introduce the fundamental concept of utilizing tokens and the technique of tokenization in NLP.

When working with natural language, it is crucial to break down text into smaller units for analysis and processing. These smaller units are known as tokens. Tokenization, on the other hand, refers to the process of splitting text into individual tokens based on certain rules or patterns. This technique is an essential preprocessing step in NLP, as it allows machines to understand and manipulate text in a structured manner.

Tokenization serves multiple purposes in NLP. Firstly, it helps us to analyze the structure of a sentence or a document. By breaking down text into tokens, we gain insights into the grammatical structure, parts of speech, and word order. These insights form the groundwork for many NLP tasks, such as parsing, entity recognition, and syntactic analysis.

Secondly, tokenization enables us to quantify and analyze the frequency and distribution of words within a text corpus. By counting tokens, we can identify common patterns, extract significant keywords, and calculate statistical measures such as word frequencies and tf-idf (term frequency-inverse document frequency). These measures are vital for tasks like text classification, topic modeling, and information retrieval.

Furthermore, tokenization plays a crucial role in improving computational efficiency and reducing the dimensionality of the data. By splitting text into tokens, we convert unstructured text into structured data that can be easily processed and modeled by machine learning algorithms. This process simplifies subsequent tasks such as feature extraction, vectorization, and model training.

As an NLP practitioner, you will encounter various challenges when tokenizing text. For instance, deciding where to split words and handling punctuation marks, abbreviations, and special characters are common obstacles. Balancing granularity, such as distinguishing between "tokens" and "types," and dealing with out-of-vocabulary words are also areas that require attention.

In the upcoming sections, we will explore different tokenization techniques, each suited for specific NLP tasks and languages. We will discuss important concepts like word tokenization, sentence tokenization, and subword tokenization. Moreover, we will examine popular tokenization libraries, tools, and algorithms used by researchers and practitioners to accomplish these tasks efficiently.

You will have a solid grasp of the importance of tokenization in NLP, the challenges associated with it, and the various techniques available to tokenize text effectively. Understanding and mastering this fundamental step will enable you to unlock the full potential of NLP, empower your applications to comprehend and process human language accurately, and lay the groundwork for more advanced NLP techniques.

**5.2 Handling Sensitive and Inappropriate Content**
As an AI research expert, I understand the importance of approaching these topics with sensitivity and caution, ensuring that individuals can use artificial intelligence in a responsible and ethical manner.

**The Reality of Sensitive and Inappropriate Content:**

In the vast digital landscape, sensitive and inappropriate content can range from explicit material to hate speech, and everything in between. As our interconnected world continues to grow, so does the presence of these materials, making it imperative for individuals to recognize and address them appropriately.

**Understanding the Impact:**

The presence of sensitive and inappropriate content can have severe consequences on individuals, societal norms, and our overall well-being. Exposure to explicit content can be distressing and harmful, particularly to vulnerable individuals such as children or those with certain psychological conditions. Moreover, inappropriate or hateful speech can perpetuate discrimination, prejudice, and even incite violence. Recognizing the impact of such content empowers us to take proactive measures in handling it responsibly.

**Addressing Sensitive and Inappropriate Content:**

**Guidelines and Policies:**
Organizations and platforms have a crucial role to play in defining guidelines and implementing policies that regulate the handling of sensitive and inappropriate content. These guidelines aim to strike a delicate balance between ensuring freedom of expression and preventing harm

caused by explicit or offensive material. Understanding and adhering to these guidelines will assist individuals in creating safe online spaces and communities.

**Moderation and Filtering:**
Various tools and techniques can aid in moderating and filtering sensitive and inappropriate content. Content filtering algorithms, for example, enable the automatic identification and removal of explicit material or hateful speech. However, it is vital to keep in mind that these techniques are not foolproof and may require human intervention to address nuanced situations effectively.

**User Reporting:**
Empowering users to report sensitive or inappropriate content provides an additional layer of protection. Platforms should have user-friendly mechanisms in place to encourage reporting and take appropriate action promptly. By fostering a culture of accountability, individuals collectively contribute to maintaining a healthy and respectful digital environment.

**Ethical Considerations:**

While tackling sensitive and inappropriate content, it is essential to uphold ethical considerations. Recognizing the importance of freedom of speech, it becomes imperative to strike a balance between safeguarding individuals from harm and promoting a diverse range of perspectives. Accountable content moderation practices ensure fairness without infringing on users' rights, fostering an inclusive online discourse.

Handling sensitive and inappropriate content can be a challenging task, but by understanding the impact, adhering to guidelines, utilizing moderation and filtering tools, encouraging user reporting, and upholding ethical considerations, individuals can actively contribute to a safer digital ecosystem. As AI technology advances, it is imperative to equip beginners with the necessary know-how to employ these measures responsibly. By doing so, we can collectively create a digital world that is respectful, inclusive, and supportive for all.

## 5.3 Analyzing and Debugging GPT-4 Chat Outputs

The development of GPT-4, the fourth iteration of the Generative Pre-trained Transformer model, has revolutionized the field of natural language processing and chatbot technologies. As with any sophisticated AI system, GPT-4 may encounter errors or produce outputs that are unexpected or undesirable. In this chapter, we delve into techniques for analyzing and debugging GPT-4 chat outputs, equipping beginners with the necessary tools to understand and address such issues effectively.

Understanding the Importance of Analyzing and Debugging:
Analyzing and debugging GPT-4 chat outputs is an indispensable step in ensuring the system's accuracy, consistency, and reliability. By thoroughly scrutinizing the outputs, we can identify potential flaws, inconsistencies, or biases present in the model's responses. For instance, GPT-4 may generate factually incorrect statements, exhibit insensitive language choices, or even produce nonsensical replies. Therefore, it becomes crucial for developers and researchers to be capable of unraveling and interpreting these outputs for further refinement.

**Analyzing GPT-4 Chat Outputs:**
**Decomposition of Outputs:**
**Breaking down the generated responses:**

Chat outputs from GPT-4 can sometimes be lengthy and complex. By breaking them down into individual sentences or meaning chunks, it becomes easier to analyze and focus on specific sections. This also allows us to identify any inconsistencies or contradictory statements within the response.

**Identifying source material:**
GPT-4 is trained on vast quantities of text data, so it can sometimes include snippets from its training corpus in its responses. These excerpts from external sources should be flagged, especially when used verbatim without appropriate attribution or quotation marks.

**Fact-Checking:**
**Implementing fact-checking systems:**
While GPT-4 is an impressive language model, it may generate responses that include inaccurate or outdated information. By integrating fact-checking systems, we can verify the factual accuracy of the generated responses. This enhances the reliability and credibility of the chatbot.

**Evaluation of sources:**

Understanding the reliability and credibility of the training data sources is crucial. Different sources can exhibit biases or present speculative information. By evaluating these sources, we can identify potential issues in the response generation process and ensure that the chatbot provides trustworthy and accurate information.

**Debugging GPT-4 Chat Outputs:**
**Fine-tuning the Model:**
### Collecting and curating user feedback:
Users often provide valuable feedback on the performance of the chatbot. By actively collecting and curating this feedback, developers can identify recurring issues and patterns. This information can guide the fine-tuning process, making the model more robust and effective.

### Experimenting with hyperparameters:
Adjusting hyperparameters, such as temperature or maximum response length, can greatly impact the output of GPT-4. By carefully experimenting with these settings, developers can optimize the chatbot's performance and address any erratic behavior.

**Filtering and Augmenting Datasets:**
### Data filtering techniques:

Pre-processing the training data is a crucial step in improving GPT-4's chat output. Filtering out biased or low-quality data helps mitigate the risk of generating inappropriate or undesirable responses.

**Augmenting datasets:**
By augmenting the training data with a diverse range of examples, we can enhance GPT-4's ability to generate more accurate and contextually appropriate responses. Techniques such as data augmentation, synthetic data generation, or incorporating user-specific data can significantly improve the model's performance.

Analyzing and debugging GPT-4 chat outputs empowers developers to enhance the accuracy, consistency, and reliability of the chatbot. By decomposing outputs, fact-checking responses, fine-tuning the model, and filtering and augmenting datasets, we can ensure that GPT-4 is optimized to produce high-quality and contextually appropriate responses. Implementing these techniques lays the foundation for the development of more refined and effective AI systems, contributing to the advancement of natural language processing and chatbot technologies as a whole.

## 5.4 Exploring Multi-Turn Conversations and Long Dialogues

Conversations, at their core, are the backbone of human interaction and language understanding. As language models have evolved, there has been an increased focus on developing systems that can engage in multi-turn conversations, simulating human-like dialogues.

Multi-turn conversations refer to dialogues that span several exchanges between two or more participants. Unlike traditional single-turn dialogue, which involves just one question or statement, multi-turn conversations add a layer of complexity and diversity to the conversation process. By exploring these extended dialogues, we not only gain a deeper understanding of human language but also challenge the capabilities of AI systems to interact in a more nuanced and context-dependent manner.

One of the primary motivations behind exploring multi-turn conversations is to build systems that can hold coherent and meaningful interactions with users. This becomes especially relevant in chatbot design, customer support services, and virtual assistant applications. By enabling computers to engage in back-and-forth exchanges, we aim to create more natural and effective communication channels.

There are various key components to consider when working with multi-turn conversations. Firstly, we need to understand the notion of context, which plays a crucial role in guiding the conversation flow. Context can be thought of as the accumulated information from previous turns that helps participants maintain coherence and relevance in their responses. By incorporating context understanding into AI models, we enable them to generate more context-aware and contextually-appropriate replies.

Another important aspect is the management of long dialogues, which can include multiple subtopics or branching paths. Addressing long dialogues requires advanced techniques such as dialogue state tracking, memory management, and conversation flow control. These techniques allow AI systems to keep track of the dialogue history, retain relevant information, and smoothly navigate through various topics or subtasks.

Furthermore, exploring multi-turn conversations opens doors to investigating the dynamics of human discourse. Conversations are not just a sequence of isolated utterances but rather a coherent exchange with shared goals, information flow, and social cues. Developing models that can capture and interpret these conversational dynamics enables us to create more engaging and empathetic AI systems.

We will discuss the role of context modeling, dialogue management techniques, and evaluation methods specific to this domain. By understanding these foundations, beginners can grasp the intricacies of building intelligent systems capable of engaging in extended and meaningful conversations.

Overall, the exploration of multi-turn conversations and long dialogues is a pivotal field within AI research that paves the way for enhanced human-computer interaction. By unlocking the ability to engage in dynamic and context-rich conversations, we open up possibilities for more natural language understanding, improved user experiences, and the creation of AI systems that can truly

comprehend and respond to the nuances of
human communication.

# Part 6: Enhancing GPT-4 Chat Performance

### 6.1 Strategies for Improving Response Accuracy

Accuracy is a fundamental aspect of AI research as it directly influences the reliability and usability of these systems in various applications.

AI systems are designed to provide responses based on the analysis of vast amounts of data and the application of complex algorithms. However, achieving high response accuracy is often a challenging task due to numerous factors such as incomplete or ambiguous data, biases in the training data, or limitations in the underlying models.

To address these challenges and improve response accuracy, researchers have developed several effective strategies. These strategies aim to overcome the inherent limitations of AI systems while ensuring reliable and trustworthy outcomes. Let's explore some of these strategies in detail:

**Data Augmentation:**
One of the prominent approaches to improving response accuracy is by augmenting the training

data. Data augmentation involves generating additional training examples by applying various transformations to the existing data. These transformations may include perturbations, noise addition, or synthetic data generation. By augmenting the dataset, AI models gain exposure to a wider range of scenarios, leading to improved generalization and enhanced accuracy.

**Transfer Learning:**
Another powerful technique to enhance response accuracy is transfer learning. Transfer learning leverages knowledge gained from training on one task to improve performance on another related task. By utilizing pre-trained models on large datasets, AI systems can benefit from the learned representations, enabling them to generalize better and produce more accurate responses even with limited task-specific data.

**Ensemble Learning:**
Ensemble learning involves combining multiple AI models to obtain a more accurate and robust response. This technique works on the principle that the collective decision of multiple models, each with its own strengths and weaknesses, yields better results than a single model alone. Ensemble methods such as bagging, boosting,

and stacking effectively reduce biases and errors, enhancing response accuracy and overall system performance.

### Adaptive Learning:

To enhance response accuracy over time, adaptive learning techniques are often employed. Adaptive learning algorithms aim to dynamically update the AI model based on new data or evolving user feedback. By continuously adapting to changing circumstances, these models can rapidly correct errors and improve their accuracy, ensuring reliable and up-to-date responses in real-time scenarios.

### Bias Mitigation:

Addressing biases is crucial for improving the fairness and accuracy of AI system responses. Bias mitigation techniques focus on identifying and reducing biases present in training data or models that may lead to biased or unfair outcomes. These techniques involve careful preprocessing, data sampling, and fine-tuning of model parameters to ensure that AI systems provide unbiased and accurate responses to different users and demographics.

### Active Learning:

Active learning is a method that aims to optimize the training process by actively selecting the most informative samples from a large unlabeled dataset. By intelligently choosing which samples to label, active learning helps AI models improve their accuracy while minimizing the manual annotation effort required. This strategy is particularly useful when labeled data is scarce, expensive, or time-consuming to acquire.

**Domain Adaptation:**
AI systems often face challenges in accurately responding to out-of-domain or unseen data. Domain adaptation techniques aim to bridge the gap between the training and deployment domains by aligning the model's representations with the target domain's data distribution. By effectively transferring knowledge from a known source domain to an unknown target domain, domain adaptation strategies can significantly enhance the accuracy of AI system responses in diverse real-world settings.

**Error Analysis and Post-processing:**
Error analysis is a fundamental step to understanding the limitations of AI models and identifying patterns of inaccuracies. By carefully analyzing prediction errors and failure cases,

researchers can finetune models, improve training data, or apply post-processing techniques to rectify inaccuracies and enhance overall system accuracy. This systematic approach helps refine AI systems, making them more reliable and effective in generating accurate responses.

By implementing and combining these strategies, AI researchers and practitioners work towards achieving higher accuracy in AI system responses. As the field advances, continuous research and innovation in these strategies will lead to further improvements, enabling AI systems to provide increasingly accurate and trustworthy outcomes for a wide range of applications.

## 6.2 Reducing Bias in GPT-4 Chat Outputs

Bias is an important concern when it comes to AI systems, including language models such as GPT-4. These models, while powerful and capable of generating human-like text, can inadvertently reflect and amplify societal biases present in the data they are trained on. As a responsible AI researcher and developer, it is essential to address and alleviate these biases, striving for fairness, inclusivity, and ethical practices in AI applications.

In this section, we delve into the topic of reducing bias specifically in GPT-4 chat outputs, highlighting various strategies and tools that can be employed to accomplish this important objective. By proactively managing and mitigating bias, we can not only improve the quality and reliability of the AI-generated content but also ensure that it aligns with the values and expectations of users.

One of the primary steps in reducing bias is to analyze and understand the sources of bias present in the training data. Biases can emerge from historical imbalances, societal stereotypes, or unintentional skewing due to data collection methods. By thoroughly examining the training dataset, developers can identify potential sources of bias and take corrective measures to curtail their impact on GPT-4's chat outputs.

Addressing bias also necessitates regular evaluation and monitoring throughout the development process. Developers should set up robust mechanisms to assess the performance of GPT-4 in real-world scenarios, detect biases, and promptly rectify any shortcomings. This continual evaluation allows for an iterative and adaptive approach, enabling developers to refine the system and make it more fair and unbiased over time.

To further reduce bias, developers can explore techniques such as counterfactual data augmentation and adversarial training. Counterfactual data augmentation involves augmenting the training dataset with hypothetical examples that challenge and mitigate biases. This technique helps GPT-4 learn to generate responses that consider a wide range of perspectives and avoid favoring a particular group or viewpoint.

Adversarial training, on the other hand, involves training GPT-4 to recognize and counter biases by engaging it in a game-like scenario. By exposing the model to biased and unbiased examples, GPT-4 learns to detect and suppress biased outputs, promoting more inclusive and equitable conversation outcomes.

Another critical aspect of reducing bias is promoting transparency and accountability. Developers should provide clear documentation on the training process, data sources, and the steps taken to address biases. This transparency helps users understand the limitations and potential biases associated with AI systems, fostering informed and responsible usage.

In addition to technical approaches, developers should also incorporate diverse and inclusive perspectives during the design, development, and deployment of GPT-4. This can be achieved by seeking input from a wide range of stakeholders, including individuals from different backgrounds, cultures, and demographics. By involving a diverse group of experts in the decision-making process, developers can proactively identify and rectify potential biases, ensuring a more balanced and unbiased system overall.

It is important to note that while significant progress can be made in reducing bias, completely eliminating bias from AI systems is an ongoing challenge. Bias often exists at multiple levels, including in the training data, the models themselves, and even in the interpretation and use of AI-generated outputs. Hence, it is vital to remain diligent and continuously improve approaches to mitigate bias as AI technologies evolve.

Reducing bias in GPT-4 chat outputs is a complex yet essential endeavor that goes hand in hand with building responsible and trustworthy AI systems. By adopting a multifaceted approach focused on understanding, evaluation, technical advancements, transparency, and diverse perspectives, developers can strive towards minimizing bias, ensuring fairness, and maximizing the benefits of AI in a manner that aligns with the values of humanity as a whole.

**6.3 Dealing with Output Consistency Issues**
In the exciting field of AI, where algorithms and models are becoming increasingly sophisticated, it is vital to ensure that the output generated by these intelligent systems is consistent, reliable, and trustworthy. Output consistency refers to the ability of an AI system to produce the same or similar results for similar inputs across different instances. However, achieving consistent outputs can be a challenging task due to various factors that can introduce inconsistencies into the system.

In this chapter, we will delve into the intricacies of dealing with output consistency issues in AI systems. We will explore the causes of these inconsistencies and provide you with practical strategies to mitigate them, enabling you to build more robust and dependable AI applications.

One of the primary reasons for output inconsistencies in AI systems is the nature of the underlying data. Data, being inherently noisy and imperfect, can lead to variations in the patterns recognized by the models. Furthermore, biases and imbalances present in the training data can result in skewed predictions, rendering the output inconsistent. Therefore, it becomes crucial to preprocess and prepare the data meticulously, ensuring its quality, balance, and representativeness.

Another factor contributing to output inconsistencies is the complexity of the models themselves. Deep learning models, for instance, often consist of multiple layers and millions of parameters that need to be optimized. Any change in these parameters during training or inference can potentially alter the output, impacting consistency. To address this, we will explore regularization techniques, such as weight decay and dropout, which can help stabilize model outputs, leading to improved consistency.

Additionally, the design and architecture of an AI system can greatly influence its output consistency. Poorly designed models, lacking in appropriate architectural choices, may yield unpredictable outputs. We will discuss various architectural considerations, including the choice of activation functions, network depth, and width, that can impact output consistency. Understanding these design principles will empower you to make informed decisions when building AI systems.

Furthermore, we will explore the concept of interpretability and its role in ensuring output consistency. By making AI models more transparent, we can gain insights into the decision-making process and detect potential sources of inconsistency. Techniques such as neural network interpretability, saliency maps, and Grad-CAM will be discussed to help you gain a deeper understanding of your AI system's behavior.

As models are deployed in dynamic real-world environments, they can encounter various sources of drift and change in the input distribution. By deploying monitoring mechanisms and leveraging techniques like A/B testing, we can detect and rectify inconsistencies, ensuring ongoing reliability of the AI system.

It aims to equip you with a comprehensive understanding of output consistency issues in AI systems and arm you with valuable techniques to mitigate them. By the end, you will possess the knowledge and skills needed to build reliable and consistent AI systems that inspire trust and deliver accurate results across different scenarios. So let's dive into the world of output consistency and take the first steps towards building robust AI systems.

## 6.4 Addressing Ethical and Legal Considerations

In our journey exploring the vast field of artificial intelligence, it is crucial to acknowledge that technological progress is not immune to ethical and legal considerations. As the impact and prevalence of AI continue to expand, it becomes increasingly important to address these concerns. In this section, we delve into the complex realm of ethical and legal considerations surrounding AI, aiming to provide beginners with a comprehensive understanding of the issues at hand.

Ethics plays a fundamental role in the development and deployment of AI systems. As AI algorithms become capable of making decisions and interacting with individuals and society, it is vital to ensure that these systems align with our moral principles. We explore the ethical dimension to AI by raising thought-provoking questions: How should AI be used in a just and fair manner? What principles should govern the development of AI technologies? How can we mitigate bias and discrimination in AI systems? These questions encourage us to critically examine the ethical implications of AI and to foster responsible practices throughout its life cycle.

One prominent ethical concern surrounding AI is the potential impact on privacy and data protection. The enormous amounts of data required to train AI models raise concerns about the security and privacy of personal information. As we delve into this subject, we will explore concepts such as data anonymization, consent, and transparency to ensure that AI systems respect and protect individuals' privacy rights.

Moreover, transparency and explainability are crucial components in addressing ethical concerns related to AI. As AI systems become more complex and sophisticated, it becomes increasingly challenging to understand their decision-making processes. The lack of transparency may lead to mistrust, hindering the widespread adoption of AI. By examining techniques such as interpretable machine learning and explainable AI, we aim to shed light on how we can make AI systems more transparent and accountable.

In addition to ethical considerations, we must also navigate the intricate labyrinth of legal issues surrounding AI. The rapid advancements in AI technology have raised questions about liability and accountability in case of errors or harm caused by AI systems. Is it the responsibility of the developer, the user, or both? How can we establish legal frameworks to address emerging challenges in this rapidly evolving field? In this section, we provide an overview of existing legislation and explore the ongoing legal debates and discussions shaping the AI landscape.

Intellectual property rights are another legal aspect that cannot be ignored when discussing AI. The development of AI often relies on vast amounts of existing data, raising questions about ownership and copyright. We will explore the complexities surrounding data rights and intellectual property, considering both the ethical and legal implications.

Furthermore, ethical concerns extend beyond the development and deployment of AI systems; they encompass the broader socioeconomic impact of AI on employment, inequality, and human well-being. We examine the implications of AI on the labor market and delve into the concept of AI ethics in the workplace. By doing so, we aim to foster a comprehensive understanding of how AI may shape our society and how we can strive for equitable and inclusive outcomes.

As we embark on this exploration of ethical and legal considerations in AI, it is important to remember that this field is continuously evolving. New challenges and questions will undoubtedly arise, necessitating ongoing discourse and continuous critical analysis. By equipping ourselves with knowledge and fostering a multidisciplinary approach to AI, we can navigate these considerations responsibly, ensuring that technology serves humanity in a beneficial and ethical manner.

# Part 7: GPT-4 Chat Best Practices

## 7.1 Structuring Engaging and Conversational Openings

Engaging and conversational openings play a pivotal role in capturing the attention and continued interest of the readers. Whether you are writing a book, an article, or even a simple social media post, mastering the art of crafting an engaging opening can greatly impact your ability to connect with your audience. In this chapter, we delve deep into the art and science of structuring openings that are lively, relatable, and bound to capture the curiosity of your readers from the very beginning.

Understanding the Importance of Openings: Imagine holding a book that leaves you intrigued and excited, directly from the first page itself. Such discoveries are intriguing and excel at establishing the intended purposes of the author. Openings serve as the foundation of any piece of writing, setting the tone, mood, and conveying the broader purpose it holds. A well-crafted beginning can act as a powerful hook, beckoning readers to dive further into the creative realm an author is about to embark upon.

Evolving Trends in Engaging Openings:
Storytelling has forever been a captivating part of human cultures since ancient times; hence, it comes as no surprise that the art of intriguing openings has transformed significantly over generations. Once reliant on the sensory all vital channel of communication, authors now harness innovative styles and structures to transcend creative boundaries and establish a deep connection with their audience. Indeed, an engaging opening embodies both familiar and exciting elements, setting a unique stage that captures the reader's attention amidst a sea of unparalleled choices.

Establishing Conversation with Openings:
Emulating natural conversation has also become an effective technique for forming deeper connections with readers. By initiating this dialogue-like atmosphere, openings harness the power of relatability and familiarity, consistently teasing readers' intellectual curiosities - a critical factor in grasping and maintaining their interests throughout.

Fundamentals of Crafting Engaging Openings: To begin, we unraveled the core elements that contribute to crafting these artful beginnings. This chapter walks you through tips and techniques that allow a blend between artistic appeal and effective communication.

Authentic Engagement: Connect authentically with your readers from the very start by conjuring feelings of empathy, surprise, or curiosity. Develop connections through shared emotions or experiences, giving your opening a relatable touch right off the bat.

Vivid Imagery: Appeal to the readers' senses and evoke visualization from the early moments of your work. Engage their imagination through descriptive language, carefully crafting engaging openings that create vivid sensory experiences and transport the reader to alternative realms or environments.

Intriguing Questions: Suspense transforms openings into irresistible magnets, extending the desire to read beyond a single chapter. Triggering curiosity via intelligent questions will play a pivotal role in keeping readers avid and motivated to explore further.

Provoking Thoughts: Carefully sculpt linguistic structures that inspire readers to question, analyse, and think deeper. With this interactive approach at the onset, engaging openings challenge readers' preconceived notions and provoke them to dive into the narrative, thirsting for plausible answers.

Human Connection: Captivating readers often involves portraying characters that exemplify various human components. Delve into emotions, conflicts, motivations, victories, or vulnerabilities, allowing readers an opportunity to resonate with the narrators or storylines.

Spontaneity and Variation: Excite readers with sprightly, unexpected prose, avoiding redundant or predictable openings. Cultivate opportunities to surprise readers craftily, maintaining an element of novelty within your written works.

Intimate Voice: Imbu a conversational undertone as you venture into your opening passage, effectively mirroring real-world exchanges. The precise tone nearly becomes a reflection of friendliness, engaging their attention and fostering an interactive bond.

By frequently employing these fundamental techniques, you will acquire the ability to consistently captivate readers through artfully constructed beginnings. Understanding the decisive impact of structure and engaging language, we collectively aim to nurture this skill and elevate opening experiences, catering to diverse audiences eager to explore the narratives you weave.

In our subsequent sections, we dissect each principle to unveil golden practices necessary to grip the attention of your readers and establish that initial connection capable of enhancing their experience of your written works immeasurably.

**7.2 Nurturing User Engagement and Retention**
User engagement refers to the level of involvement, interaction, and attention users invest in a digital product or service. Retention, on the other hand, focuses on maintaining a user's continued and prolonged association with the product or service. Both engagement and retention are essential for the sustainable growth and success of any digital entity.

**Understanding User Engagement:**
First, we explore the concept of user engagement in its entirety. We discuss various metrics and indicators that help measure and analyze engagement levels effectively. Some of these metrics include the number of active users, session duration, frequency of interactions, and rates of returning users. By understanding the quantitative and qualitative aspects of user engagement, beginners can gauge the success and effectiveness of their digital offerings.

**Driving User Engagement:**
Next, we delve into proven strategies and techniques to drive user engagement. We examine the importance of creating seamless user experiences, such as intuitive interfaces, fast loading speeds, and personalized content. Through clear and concise communication, beginners are taught how to effectively convey the value proposition of their products or services to users. Additionally, we emphasize the significance of incentivizing user actions, implementing gamification techniques, and fostering a sense of community to enhance engagement levels.

**Retention Strategies:**

After establishing a solid foundation in user engagement, we shift our focus to user retention. We explore the reasons behind user churn, their motivations, and how to pinpoint critical moments that lead to attrition. Beginners will learn how to develop effective onboarding processes to ensure users have a positive initial experience, thus increasing the chances of long-term retention. Furthermore, we discuss the importance of regularly updating and improving digital products or services to keep users engaged and interested.

**The Role of Data Analysis:**
Throughout this chapter, we emphasize the significance of data analysis and its impact on user engagement and retention. We guide beginners in leveraging analytical tools to gain insights into user behavior, preferences, and patterns. By employing data-driven decision-making processes, businesses can optimize their strategies to deliver personalized experiences and effectively retain users in the highly competitive digital ecosystem.

In this detailed chapter, beginners are provided with valuable insights and actionable strategies to nurture user engagement and support long-term user retention. By thoroughly understanding the principles discussed in this chapter, readers will be equipped to shape their digital products or services to attract, engage, and retain a loyal user base. Implementing these strategies will not only drive growth and success but also foster strong, meaningful connections between businesses and their users in the dynamic world of digital technology.

### 7.3 Maintaining a Cohesive and Natural Dialogue Flow

In the realm of artificial intelligence, dialogue systems have revolutionized the way humans interact with machines. These systems aim to provide seamless and natural conversations, making users feel as if they are engaging with another human being rather than a machine. However, achieving a cohesive and natural dialogue flow is a complex task that requires careful attention to various aspects of dialogue management.

One of the fundamental challenges in maintaining a cohesive dialogue flow is context tracking. Context refers to the collective information that frames a conversation. A well-designed dialogue system should be able to keep track of this information to ensure meaningful and coherent interactions. Context tracking involves understanding and preserving relevant information such as user preferences, previous system responses, and any ongoing tasks or goals. By maintaining a robust context, the dialogue system can generate responses that are relevant and consistent, building a sense of continuity within the conversation.

To achieve a natural dialogue flow, proper turn-taking is crucial. Just like in a conversation between two humans, dialogue systems need to have a clear understanding of when to respond and when to listen. Turn-taking involves accurately identifying the end of a user's turn and seamlessly transitioning to the system's turn. This requires sophisticated techniques to detect the completion of a user's utterance, including detecting pauses, sentence boundaries, and other cues. By ensuring smooth turn-taking, the dialogue system can avoid awkward interruptions or delays, contributing to a more natural and engaging conversation.

Furthermore, maintaining coherence within a dialogue involves generating responses that are not only relevant but also contextually appropriate. This entails considering the current context, including the user's latest query, the system's previous responses, and any contextual information from previous turns. A cohesive dialogue flow is achieved by generating responses that make logical sense within the ongoing conversation and align with the user's expectations. Careful attention must be given to contextual dependencies, as overlooking them can lead to misleading or irrelevant responses, undermining the overall coherence of the dialogue.

To enhance dialogue flow, techniques like dialogue state tracking can be employed. Dialogue state tracking involves modeling the state of the conversation, keeping track of various dialogue attributes such as user intents, slots, and system actions. By continuously updating and refining this dialogue state, the system can make informed decisions about generating appropriate and coherent responses. An accurate dialogue state representation enables the system to understand the user's goals and preferences, thereby tailoring the conversation to their specific needs.

In addition to maintaining the flow of dialogue, it is essential to actively engage users throughout the conversation. Engagement encourages users to continue interacting with the system and helps create a more satisfying user experience. Techniques like proactive suggestions, personalized responses, and empathetic language can all contribute to higher user engagement. Carefully understanding user feedback and incorporating it into the dialogue system's design can also enhance engagement and improve overall satisfaction.

To summarize, maintaining a cohesive and natural dialogue flow is a multidimensional challenge that requires diligent attention to context tracking, turn-taking, coherence, dialogue state tracking, and user engagement. By carefully considering and addressing these aspects, dialogue systems can create more meaningful and interactive conversations, blurring the lines between human-human and human-machine communication. As technology continues to advance, so too will the capabilities of dialogue systems, bringing us closer to a future where AI-driven conversations are indistinguishable from those we have with fellow humans.

## 7.4 Evaluating and Iterating on GPT-4 Chat Performance

In our quest to develop reliable and intelligent conversational agents, evaluating the performance of AI models is crucial. In this chapter, we delve into the details of how we assess and improve the chat performance of GPT-4, a cutting-edge language model.

As AI researchers and practitioners, it is essential for us to measure the effectiveness and robustness of our models in order to refine and enhance their capabilities. Evaluating chat performance involves a meticulous process of analyzing both quantitative and qualitative metrics, which help us gauge the quality, coherence, and relevance of the responses generated by GPT-4.

Quantitative evaluation provides us with statistical measurements of the model's performance. One widely used metric is perplexity, which calculates how well the model predicts the next token in a conversation. A lower perplexity score indicates that the model has a better grasp of the conversational context and generates more coherent responses. We also evaluate response length, as overly verbose replies can be counterproductive, while excessively brief responses may lack necessary information. By studying these quantitative metrics, we can objectively identify areas for improvement in GPT-4's chat performance.

However, quantitative evaluation alone may not capture the intricacies of human-like conversation. Thus, qualitative evaluation becomes equally important. Engaging human evaluators to provide subjective feedback on conversations generated by GPT-4 enables us to assess the model's fluency, relevance, and ability to sustain coherent dialogues. This valuable input helps identify potential biases, logical inconsistencies, or other limitations of the system. It is crucial to continuously iterate and refine the model based on this qualitative evaluation to ensure that GPT-4 aligns better with human conversation norms.

Iterative improvement is a core element of developing GPT-4's chat performance. Leveraging both automatic metrics and human feedback, we can explore various approaches to address weaknesses and enhance conversational abilities over time. By continuously fine-tuning the model and feeding it with abundantly diverse training data, we aim to achieve more accurate, contextual, and natural responses. Integrating ongoing evaluation and iteration cycles into the development process helps us close the gap between current AI capabilities and the desired human-level conversation experience.

Moreover, it is crucial to ensure that GPT-4 respects ethical standards, maintains neutral positions, and refrains from promoting harmful content. Evaluating and iterating on chat performance encompasses not only enhancing the model's linguistic capabilities but also ensuring its responsible deployment and adherence to ethical guidelines.

By carefully assessing and iteratively improving the chat performance of GPT-4, we aim to develop more reliable and trustworthy conversational agents that can seamlessly interact with humans. Through a combination of quantitative metrics, human evaluators, and continuous iteration, we strive to create AI systems that emulate human-like conversations while addressing limitations and biases, ultimately contributing to the advancement of the field and promoting responsible AI deployment.

It provides a comprehensive exploration of the evaluation and iteration processes employed to enhance the chat performance of GPT-4. By understanding the intricacies involved in evaluating conversational AI models, we equip ourselves with the knowledge and tools necessary for future advancements in this exciting domain.

# Part 8: Future Developments and Challenges

## 8.1 Anticipated Advancements in AI-Language Models

Artificial Intelligence (AI) has been rapidly advancing in recent years and has become increasingly prevalent in various fields, revolutionizing how we perform tasks, interact with technology, and communicate with each other. One particularly exciting area of AI development is language modeling, which focuses on the ability of AI systems to understand, generate, and respond to human language in a meaningful and coherent way.

We will explore the anticipated advancements in AI-language models, providing you with a comprehensive overview of the cutting-edge research and technology that is driving this field forward. These anticipated advancements hold the potential to unlock a new era of AI capabilities, enabling machines to grasp language nuances, context, and even emotions, resulting in more natural and human-like communication.

Improved Language Understanding: Current language models have made significant progress in tasks such as text completion, translation, and sentiment analysis. However, they still struggle to fully comprehend complex language structures, idiomatic expressions, and contextual ambiguity. Anticipated advancements in AI-language models aim to overcome these limitations by developing models that not only process individual words but also capture semantic relationships, infer meanings, and utilize contextual cues effectively.

Enhanced Contextual Understanding: AI-language models are being designed to better understand and respond to the context in which language is presented. Currently, most models handle utterances as isolated instances without considering previous or subsequent text. Anticipated advancements seek to develop language models that can maintain a coherent and consistent understanding of the context, enabling them to generate more accurate and relevant responses.

Multi-modal Communication: While humans communicate using various channels, including spoken language, written text, facial expressions, and gestures, AI systems have primarily focused on text-based interactions. Future advancements aim to enable AI-language models to process and incorporate multiple modalities, such as images, videos, and audio, into their understanding and generation of language. This would result in more comprehensive and immersive communication experiences.

Few-shot and Zero-shot Learning: Currently, language models require extensive training with large amounts of labeled data to perform well across different tasks. Anticipated advancements in AI-language models aim to reduce the need for such extensive training by enabling models to generalize from limited data (few-shot learning) or even perform adequately on tasks for which they have not been explicitly trained (zero-shot learning). This would greatly increase the flexibility and adaptability of AI systems in handling a wide range of language-based tasks.

Ethical Considerations: As AI-language models become more sophisticated and capable, the importance of addressing ethical concerns becomes paramount. The anticipated advancements include developing models that are more transparent, accountable, and unbiased.

Researchers are actively working towards mitigating biases, identifying and rectifying potential pitfalls, and ensuring that the models maintain compliance with ethical standards.

By immersing yourself in this section, you will gain insights into the exciting advancements on the horizon for AI-language models. From improved language understanding to enhanced contextual comprehension, and from multi-modal communication to more efficient learning techniques, the anticipated advancements are set to significantly elevate the capabilities of AI systems in understanding and generating human language. Let us now embark on this journey together and explore the limitless potential of AI in the realm of language.

## 8.2 Ethical and Societal Implications of GPT-4 Chat

As we delve deeper into the world of artificial intelligence (AI), it becomes increasingly important to address the ethical and societal implications that arise with the development and deployment of powerful AI systems. In this section, we will explore the potential impact of GPT-4 Chat, a cutting-edge language model that has the ability to carry out natural and seamless conversations with users.

GPT-4 Chat is the fourth iteration of the popular Generative Pre-trained Transformer (GPT) series developed by OpenAI. It is designed to understand and generate human-like text responses, making it incredibly useful in various applications such as customer service, virtual assistants, and content creation. This latest version boasts significant improvements over its predecessors, displaying even more natural language understanding and generation capabilities.

However, with every leap in technology comes a responsibility to carefully evaluate the ethical implications it brings. GPT-4 Chat represents a significant advancement in AI technology, and as such, it presents both opportunities and challenges for society. In this section, we will explore some of these critical implications to foster a better understanding of the potential effects GPT-4 Chat may have on individuals and communities.

One important consideration is the potential for misinformation and manipulation. Given GPT-4

Chat's ability to generate highly plausible text, there is a risk of it being misused to spread false information or engage in malicious activities such as phishing or impersonation. Such misuse could have detrimental effects on individuals, organizations, and even democratic processes, as false narratives can quickly spread and influence public opinion.

Another crucial area of concern lies in the preservation of privacy and data security. GPT-4 Chat relies on vast amounts of data to learn and generate responses. While efforts are made to anonymize and protect user data, there is always a possibility of unintended data leaks or breaches. Striking a balance between personalized user experiences and protecting individual privacy is a challenge that must be navigated carefully to ensure user trust and confidence.

Furthermore, the impact of GPT-4 Chat on human labor and employment cannot be ignored. The integration of highly capable AI chat systems in various industries may lead to workforce reductions or shifts in job roles. While AI can automate repetitive tasks and enhance efficiency, it is essential to ensure that adequate support and retraining opportunities are available for those affected by these changes. Broader societal implications, such as income inequality and potential job displacement, need to be addressed to ensure a fair transition.

Ethical considerations tied to bias and fairness are also pertinent when examining AI systems like GPT-4 Chat. These models learn from vast amounts of data, which can inadvertently incorporate societal biases present in the training data. As a result, GPT-4 Chat may unintentionally perpetuate stereotypes or exhibit discriminatory behavior. Recognizing and mitigating such bias is crucial to developing AI systems that treat all individuals equitably.

As we navigate the ethical and societal implications of GPT-4 Chat and similar AI technologies, it is crucial to engage in open and inclusive conversations involving experts, policymakers, and the wider public. This broad participation allows for diverse perspectives to be considered and informs the development of appropriate regulations, guidelines, and frameworks that govern the use of such powerful AI systems.

The advent of GPT-4 Chat has the potential to revolutionize human-computer interactions and transform various industries. However, it also raises important ethical and societal questions that must be carefully examined. By addressing concerns related to misinformation, privacy, labor displacement, bias, and fairness, we can utilize this advanced technology responsibly and ensure that it benefits humanity as a whole.

**8.3 Potential Limitations and Challenges of GPT-4**

GPT-4, the fourth iteration of the popular Generative Pre-trained Transformer model, is no exception. In this section, we will explore the potential drawbacks and obstacles that could arise with the deployment of GPT-4, shedding light on areas that require careful consideration and ongoing research.

One of the primary concerns surrounding GPT-4 revolves around ethical considerations and responsible use. As AI systems become increasingly capable of generating text that appears highly human-like, the risk of misuse or malicious exploitation rises. GPT-4 could be used to spread misinformation, produce fake news at an unprecedented scale, or even engage in malicious activities such as generating harmful content or participating in illicit activities. Therefore, it is crucial for developers, policymakers, and users to establish guidelines and regulations to ensure responsible deployment and usage of AI systems like GPT-4, to prevent any potential harm to individuals or society.

Another potential limitation of GPT-4 is the issue of bias in the generated output. AI models are trained on vast amounts of data, often sourced from the internet, which might contain biased content. Consequently, GPT-4 could inadvertently produce biased or discriminatory text, further amplifying the existing social and cultural biases prevalent in our society. Tackling this challenge requires ongoing efforts to develop mechanisms for debiasing the training data and building methods into the system to detect and mitigate biased outputs. This remains an active area of research in the field of AI ethics.

The sheer computational requirements of GPT-4 can pose a significant challenge. As AI models grow larger and more complex, they demand substantial computational power and resources to train and deploy effectively. Training GPT-4 would require immensely powerful hardware infrastructure, which can be logistically and financially burdensome for many organizations or individuals. Additionally, the energy consumption of such models is high, highlighting concerns about their environmental impact. Developers must find ways to optimize these models, making them more efficient and accessible without compromising their performance.

The issue of explainability and transparency is yet another challenge associated with GPT-4. While GPT-4 may generate impressive text, understanding the internal workings of the model and the reasoning behind its output can be difficult. This lack of interpretability makes it challenging to trust and rely on AI-generated results, especially in critical applications like medicine or law. Efforts must be made to develop explainable AI models, ensuring transparency and allowing users to comprehend how decisions are made, enabling better adoption and reducing potential mistrust.

Furthermore, GPT-4 might encounter difficulties with understanding and generating context-specific text. Although it can generate coherent and contextually relevant responses in a broad range of topics, it may struggle with more nuanced or domain-specific content. This limitation might hinder its usefulness in certain specialized domains, where precise and accurate information is crucial. Addressing this challenge requires continued research and improvement in natural language understanding and training strategies to account for diverse specialized domains.

Lastly, the ethical debate surrounding data privacy and security cannot be overlooked while discussing the potential limitations of GPT-4. The training data used to train AI models like GPT-4 often comprises sensitive and personal information, making data privacy a critical concern. Ensuring that user data is handled responsibly and protected against unauthorized access or misuse is paramount. Striking a balance between the need for data-driven AI advancements and preserving privacy rights is a complex challenge that will require collaboration between tech companies, policymakers, and AI researchers.

While GPT-4 undoubtedly represents a significant milestone in AI research and development, it is crucial to acknowledge and navigate its potential limitations and challenges. Addressing ethical concerns, minimizing bias, optimizing computational requirements, enhancing explainability, improving context specificity, and safeguarding data privacy are key areas that demand continual focus and innovation. By proactively tackling these issues, we can foster the responsible and beneficial integration of GPT-4 into various domains, ushering in a future where AI technologies enhance human lives without compromising ethical values or societal well-being.

# Part 9: Case Studies and Real-World Examples

### 9.1 Industry-Specific Applications of GPT-4 Chat

As artificial intelligence continues to advance, it has become increasingly capable of understanding and generating human-like text. One of the most prominent examples of this progress is the development of GPT-4 Chat, an advanced conversational AI system that utilizes the powerful GPT (Generative Pre-trained Transformer) model. GPT-4 Chat has emerged as a game-changer in various industries, offering a wide range of applications that transform how businesses interact with their customers and stakeholders.

The GPT-4 Chat system facilitates dynamic and natural conversations while maintaining an empathetic and contextually aware demeanor. This unique capability opens up immense possibilities for numerous sectors, revolutionizing customer service, support, and even enhancing decision-making processes.

One of the areas where GPT-4 Chat has demonstrated exceptional potential is in the retail industry. By integrating this conversational AI tool into their customer service operations, retail businesses can provide personalized and efficient support to online shoppers. GPT-4 Chat can address customer queries, make product recommendations, and assist in navigating through purchase decisions. By simulating human-like conversation, GPT-4 Chat can foster strong customer engagement and enhance customer satisfaction, ultimately leading to increased sales and brand loyalty.

Moreover, the healthcare sector has also recognized the transformative power of GPT-4 Chat. With its advanced language understanding capabilities, GPT-4 Chat can assist healthcare providers in offering remote consultations and medical advice. Patients can engage in natural conversations with the AI system, discussing symptoms, receiving relevant information, and even scheduling appointments. GPT-4 Chat's ability to handle a vast amount of medical knowledge helps optimize healthcare services, streamline workflows, and enhance patient outcomes.

The finance industry, too, has experienced significant advancements with the integration of GPT-4 Chat. Chatbots powered by GPT-4 can provide comprehensive financial assistance, answering queries related to banking, investments, and financial planning. These AI-powered chat assistants can provide real-time updates on stock prices, assist in portfolio management, and even generate personalized investment recommendations based on individual goals and risk appetite. GPT-4 Chat's ability to understand complex financial jargon and provide relevant information makes it an invaluable tool for both financial institutions and their clients.

Another important application of GPT-4 Chat lies in the education sector. Incorporating GPT-4 Chat into e-learning platforms can enhance the learning experience for students. The system can act as a virtual tutor, offering personalized guidance, answering questions, and explaining complex concepts. By creating an interactive learning environment, GPT-4 Chat can help students overcome challenges, foster independent learning, and ensure a more engaging educational journey.

Furthermore, GPT-4 Chat has shown great promise in the travel and hospitality industry. By integrating this AI system into booking platforms and websites, businesses can provide customers with instant and knowledgeable support. GPT-4 Chat can assist users in finding the ideal accommodations, suggesting travel itineraries, and providing up-to-date information on travel restrictions and safety guidelines. The conversational nature of GPT-4 Chat ensures that customers receive a seamless and personalized experience, increasing their overall satisfaction and trust in the brand.

GPT-4 Chat is not just a revolutionary conversational AI system but a transformative force across various industries. The powerful capabilities of GPT-4 Chat have the potential to redefine customer interactions, streamline operations, and enhance decision-making processes. As we explore the industry-specific applications of GPT-4 Chat in this chapter, it becomes evident that the future of business interactions is increasingly reliant on the power of AI-driven conversational systems.

## 9.2 Success Stories and Best Practices from Industry Leaders

By learning from the experiences and accomplishments of these pioneers, beginners like you can gain invaluable insights into the practical applications and approaches that are shaping the AI landscape today.

As the AI industry continues to evolve at an astonishing pace, it becomes crucial to understand the strategies and methodologies that have propelled some organizations and individuals to the forefront of this rapidly advancing field. Whether you are a professional embarking on an AI-related career or a curious soul eager to explore the possibilities of AI, the real-life examples and best practices outlined in this chapter will serve as a guiding light throughout your journey.

The success stories presented here are not limited to any specific sector or domain. Instead, we have endeavored to compile a diverse array of case studies from industries such as healthcare, finance, manufacturing, transportation, and retail, among others. This breadth of examples ensures that no matter your area of interest, you will find practical applications and insights relevant to your aspirations.

Within these success stories, you will discover how companies and individuals have harnessed the power of AI to solve complex problems, streamline operations, enhance customer experiences, and drive innovation. Each case study highlights the unique challenges faced by these industry leaders and the AI solutions they deployed to overcome them. By delving into their journeys, you will gain a nuanced understanding of the possibilities and pitfalls associated with AI implementation.

To further enhance your learning experience, we have also included detailed best practices shared by these industry leaders. These insights have been distilled from years of experience and experimentation, providing you with invaluable advice as you embark on your own AI projects. From key considerations during project planning to the importance of data quality and the ethical implications of AI, these best practices equip you with the knowledge to navigate the complex landscape of AI implementation successfully.

Furthermore, throughout this chapter, you will find practical tips, tools, and frameworks that have proven effective for industry leaders. By incorporating these suggestions into your AI projects, you can increase your chances of achieving success, avoid common pitfalls, and iterate more efficiently. Remember, AI is a rapidly evolving domain, and adopting proven best practices can help you stay ahead of the curve and ensure your efforts align with current industry standards.

By studying and emulating the accomplishments of these pioneers, you gain a comprehensive understanding of the potential and practical applications of AI. Each success story provides insights into the challenges faced and the AI solutions applied, while the best practices offer a roadmap to navigate the intricacies of AI implementation. By employing the knowledge gained from this chapter, you will be better equipped to embark on your own AI journey and drive innovation in your chosen domain.

# Part 10: Conclusion and Next Steps

### 10.1 Recap of Key Takeaways

As we dive deeper into the world of AI, it is important to periodically summarize and refresh the knowledge we have acquired thus far. This section will serve as a comprehensive recap of the key takeaways from our exploration, ensuring that we have a solid understanding of the fundamental concepts before moving forward.

### What is Artificial Intelligence (AI)?

Artificial Intelligence refers to the capability of machines to simulate human intelligence, enabling them to learn, reason, and solve problems autonomously. It encompasses various academic disciplines and techniques such as machine learning, natural language processing (NLP), computer vision, robotics, and more.

### Machine Learning (ML)

Machine Learning is one of the core components of AI that focuses on developing algorithms and models that allow machines to learn from data and improve their performance over time. It involves training a model on a large dataset to recognize patterns and make predictions or decisions based on that learning.

**Supervised Learning**
Supervised Learning is a branch of ML where the model is trained using labeled examples. These examples consist of input data paired with the correct output, giving the model a clear understanding of the relationship between the two and enabling it to predict outcomes for new, unseen data.

**Unsupervised Learning**
Unsupervised Learning, on the other hand, involves training ML models without labeled data. Instead of providing explicit outputs, unsupervised learning algorithms seek to identify patterns and structures within the input data, allowing the model to recognize similarities or groupings.

**Reinforcement Learning**
Reinforcement Learning is a type of ML where an agent learns to interact with an environment over time. Through a system of rewards and punishments, the agent explores different actions and learns to take the most optimal ones to

maximize the overall reward. This approach has been extremely useful in developing intelligent systems for games, robotics, and resource allocation.

**Neural Networks**
Neural Networks are computational models inspired by the structure and functionality of biological brains. They consist of interconnected layers of artificial neurons that enable complex data processing, feature extraction, and decision-making. Deep Learning, a subfield of ML, heavily relies on neural networks to solve intricate problems.

**Natural Language Processing (NLP)**
NLP is a specialized field of AI that focuses on enabling machines to understand, interpret, and generate human language. It encompasses tasks such as speech recognition, language translation, sentiment analysis, and text generation, contributing to the development of chatbots, virtual assistants, and automated language processing systems.

**Computer Vision**
Computer Vision involves the application of AI techniques to analyze and comprehend visual

data, such as images and videos. By leveraging advanced algorithms, computer vision enables machines to recognize objects, detect motion, understand scenes, and even perform facial recognition.

## Ethics and Limitations of AI

As AI continues to progress, it is crucial to consider the ethical implications and limitations associated with its implementation. Areas such as bias in data, privacy concerns, and potential job displacement must be addressed to ensure the responsible and beneficial application of AI technologies.

## Future Trends and Opportunities

The field of AI is ever-evolving, with exciting trends and opportunities on the horizon. These include advancements in autonomous vehicles, healthcare, smart devices, augmented reality, and the fusion of AI with other emerging technologies such as blockchain and Internet of Things (IoT).

By revisiting these key takeaways, we solidify our understanding of the topics we have covered and prepare ourselves for the chapters ahead. Armed with this foundation, we will delve into more advanced concepts, algorithms, and practical applications of AI, equipping us with the knowledge and skills needed to navigate the fascinating world of artificial intelligence with confidence and enthusiasm.

## 10.2 Recommendations for Further Exploration

Artificial intelligence, with its limitless potential, offers countless opportunities for exploration. As you embark on this path, let us outline a range of recommendations that will facilitate your continued growth and comprehension of AI.

Stay Informed:
To stay at the forefront of AI research, it is crucial to keep yourself updated with the latest trends and breakthroughs in the field. Subscribe to reputable AI journals, conferences, and online platforms dedicated to AI news and research papers. Engage in discussions with fellow AI enthusiasts to exchange ideas and broaden your knowledge.

Expand your Horizons:
While building a strong foundation is essential, exploring related disciplines can lend valuable insights into AI. Consider delving into fields such as machine learning, computer vision, natural language processing, robotics, and data science.

Expanding your horizons and acquiring multidisciplinary knowledge will equip you with a broader perspective on AI's possibilities.

Hands-On Experience:
Practical experience is pivotal for honing your AI skills. Actively seek out opportunities to engage in coding projects, implement AI algorithms, and work with real-world datasets. Online platforms and coding competitions can facilitate hands-on learning and allow you to apply theoretical concepts to practical scenarios.

Collaborate and Network:
Collaboration with like-minded individuals and experts in the field can significantly enhance your understanding of AI. Join AI communities, attend meetups, and participate in forums and online groups to connect with individuals sharing similar interests. Collaborative projects expose you to diverse approaches and foster an exchange of knowledge, propelling your growth as an AI practitioner.

Explore Research Papers:
Delve into research papers authored by leading AI researchers, institutions, and organizations. Studying these papers will deepen your

understanding of cutting-edge AI techniques, algorithms, and the current state-of-the-art. Analyze their methodologies, experimental setups, and results to gain insights into innovative AI advancements.

Pursue Higher Education:
Consider pursuing advanced education in AI through specialized degree programs, such as a master's or Ph.D. degree in artificial intelligence or related fields. Higher education provides an in-depth understanding of advanced AI concepts, access to research opportunities, and guidance from seasoned academicians. It lays a strong foundation for a career in AI research or industry.

Contribute to Open Source Projects:
Engaging in open source AI initiatives allows you to contribute to the wider AI community while refining your skills. Choose projects that align with your interests and skill level, and actively participate in their development. By collaborating with experienced contributors, receiving feedback on your work, and learning from others, you will accelerate your growth as an AI practitioner.

Ethical Considerations:

As AI continues to advance, understanding the ethical implications of its applications becomes increasingly vital. Familiarize yourself with ethical frameworks and guidelines surrounding AI development and deployment. Explore the societal impact of AI, including issues of bias, privacy, transparency, and accountability, ensuring responsible AI practices in any project you undertake.

Lifelong Learning:
Recognize that AI is an ever-evolving field, constantly evolving with new technologies, algorithms, and challenges. Cultivate a mindset of lifelong learning to adapt and keep pace with these advancements. Continuously acquire new skills, stay updated with emerging research, and embrace continuous professional development to remain relevant and valuable in the AI landscape.

Embrace Real-World Challenges:
To truly master AI, it is essential to apply your skills to real-world challenges. Seek out opportunities to collaborate with industry experts, startups, or research institutions on AI projects. Tackling real-world problems will expose you to the complexities of AI implementation and

provide invaluable experience that can shape your AI journey further.

By following these recommendations, you will create a strong foundation for your continued exploration of artificial intelligence. You will be equipped to contribute to its advancements, address real-world challenges, and make a positive impact in a world where AI-driven technologies are increasingly pervasive. Harness your newfound knowledge, passion, and determination to embark on an exciting and rewarding journey in the realm of artificial intelligence.

**10.3 Inspiring Future Directions for AI-Language Models**

The world of artificial intelligence (AI) has witnessed remarkable advancements in recent years, and one of the most groundbreaking areas within this field is AI-language models. These models, powered by complex algorithms and deep learning techniques, exhibit exceptional capabilities in understanding, generating, and manipulating human language. In this chapter, we delve into the exciting possibilities and potential future directions for AI-language models, exploring the ways in which these remarkable technologies can evolve and shape various industries.

Enhancing Natural Language Understanding: AI-language models have made significant progress in comprehending and interpreting human language, but there are still areas that can be improved upon. Future directions for AI-language models involve enhancing their natural language understanding capabilities by incorporating more extensive contextual knowledge, recognizing subtler nuances within language, and understanding complex linguistic structures. This will enable AI systems to understand human language with greater accuracy and adaptability, facilitating more effective human-machine interactions.

Contextual Responsiveness:
Building upon the foundation of natural language understanding, it is crucial for AI-language models to develop contextual responsiveness. Future developments should enable AI systems to understand not only individual words or phrases but also the broader context of a conversation. By considering the conversation history and applying context-based reasoning, AI-language models can better grasp user intent,

provide more relevant responses, and engage in meaningful and coherent conversations.

Multi-modal Integration:
Expanding the capabilities of AI-language models to encompass multi-modal integration represents another exciting direction for future advancements. This involves integrating various forms of data, such as images, videos, and audio, into the linguistic frameworks of AI models. With this integration, AI systems will be able to process multi-modal information, understand visual and auditory cues, and generate rich and contextualized language-based responses. This can greatly enhance applications such as image captioning, video summarization, and interactive virtual assistants.

Explainability and Ethics:
As AI-language models become more sophisticated and integrated into various aspects of our lives, ensuring their transparency, explainability, and ethical use becomes paramount. Future research should focus on developing methods to make AI systems more interpretable, enabling users to understand the reasoning behind their responses and decisions. Furthermore, ethical considerations should be at

the forefront of AI development, addressing biases, privacy concerns, and the responsible deployment of AI-language models in order to maximize their benefits while minimizing potential risks.

Lifelong Learning and Adaptability:
AI-language models have largely relied on pre-training with massive amounts of data, followed by fine-tuning for specific tasks. However, a future direction lies in developing models capable of lifelong learning and continuous adaptation. By enabling AI systems to learn from new data and experiences, they can keep up with evolving language patterns, emerging concepts, and changing user preferences. This adaptability ensures that AI-language models remain relevant and effective in a rapidly evolving linguistic landscape.

Collaboration and Human-in-the-Loop Systems:
Building AI systems with strong collaboration and human-in-the-loop capabilities is another promising direction for exploring the potential of AI-language models. Rather than considering AI as a replacement for human intelligence, this approach emphasizes the partnership between humans and AI. Future developments should aim

to enhance AI's ability to understand and learn from user feedback, actively seek human input when faced with uncertainty, and serve as a supportive tool to augment human creativity, productivity, and decision-making.

By embracing these inspiring future directions, the field of AI-language models holds immense promise for transforming various industries, such as healthcare, education, customer service, journalism, and entertainment. As AI continues to develop and evolve, it is crucial for researchers, practitioners, and policymakers to work collaboratively towards harnessing the power of AI-language models responsibly, ethically, and for the betterment of society. This chapter offers a glimpse into the exciting possibilities that lie ahead, guiding readers towards a deeper understanding of the potential future trajectories for AI-language models.

# Appendices:

## A. GPT-4 Chat Glossary

In the world of artificial intelligence (AI), natural language processing (NLP) models have revolutionized the way we interact with technology. GPT-4, or Generative Pre-trained Transformer 4, is the latest iteration of OpenAI's advanced NLP model. It enables chat-based conversations that mimic human-like responses across various domains and topics. This glossary aims to provide beginners with a comprehensive understanding of the terminologies frequently encountered when using GPT-4 for chat-based applications.

1. AI (Artificial Intelligence): AI refers to the simulation of human-like intelligence in machines, allowing them to perform tasks that typically require human intelligence, such as understanding and generating human language.

2. NLP (Natural Language Processing): NLP is a subfield of AI that focuses on the interaction between computers and human language. It involves tasks like text-to-speech conversion,

sentiment analysis, language translation, and chat-based conversation.

3. Chatbot: A chatbot is an AI-powered software application that can engage in conversational interactions with users, simulating human conversation through text or voice-based interfaces. GPT-4 is an example of a chatbot.

4. GPT-4 (Generative Pre-trained Transformer 4): GPT-4 is a state-of-the-art language model developed by OpenAI. It uses deep learning techniques and large-scale training data to generate human-like responses in chat-based conversations.

5. Deep Learning: Deep learning is a subset of machine learning that involves training neural networks with multiple layers to learn and make predictions from data. GPT-4 utilizes deep learning algorithms to improve its language generation capabilities.

6. Neural Network: A neural network is a computer system inspired by the human brain's structure and functioning. It consists of interconnected nodes (neurons) organized in

layers. Neural networks are a fundamental component of deep learning models like GPT-4.

7. Training Data: Training data is the information used to train an AI model like GPT-4. It typically consists of vast amounts of text data from diverse sources, enabling the model to learn patterns, language nuances, and contextual information.

8. Fine-tuning: Fine-tuning is the process of customizing a pre-trained AI model, such as GPT-4, on specific data to improve its performance on specific tasks or domains. Fine-tuning involves providing additional domain-specific data and fine-tuning the model's parameters.

9. Human-in-the-Loop: Human-in-the-Loop refers to a feedback loop where human involvement is included in the training or application of an AI model. In the case of GPT-4, human-in-the-loop ensures quality control and minimizes the risk of generating inappropriate or biased responses.

10. Prompt Engineering: Prompt engineering involves carefully crafting the initial message or prompt given to GPT-4 to elicit accurate and meaningful responses. Writing clear and specific

prompts is crucial to obtaining the desired results from the chatbot.

11. User Utterance: User utterance refers to the input or message provided by the user to GPT-4 during a chat-based conversation. The accuracy and contextuality of user utterances play a crucial role in determining the chatbot's response.

12. API (Application Programming Interface): An API is a set of rules and protocols that allow different software applications to communicate with each other. GPT-4 can be accessed and utilized by developers through an API, enabling its integration into various applications.

Understanding these terminologies will enhance your journey as you delve into the exciting world of GPT-4 and chatbot development. Familiarizing yourself with these concepts sets a strong foundation for effectively utilizing this powerful tool for natural language-based applications. In the subsequent chapters, we will explore practical use cases, best practices, and strategies to make the most out of GPT-4's capabilities. So let's continue our journey and unlock the potential of AI-powered chat-based interactions!

**B. Frequently Asked Questions (FAQs)**

In an effort to provide comprehensive and accessible knowledge about the fascinating field of AI research, this book has been carefully crafted to offer beginners a solid foundation. As you embark on this journey, it's natural to have questions and seek clarification on various concepts and terms. This section aims to address some of the most commonly asked questions related to AI, shedding light on its intricacies and demystifying any uncertainties you may have.

1. What is AI?
Artificial Intelligence (AI) refers to the field of computer science focused on creating intelligent machines that can perform tasks that typically require human intelligence. It involves developing algorithms and models that enable machines to learn, reason, problem-solve, and make decisions independently, simulating human-like cognitive processes and behavior.

2. How does AI work?
AI relies on advanced algorithms and models that process vast amounts of data to recognize patterns, make predictions, and derive insights.

Machine learning, a subset of AI, involves training models on data to identify patterns and make accurate predictions without explicitly being programmed. This allows AI systems to continuously improve their performance over time.

3. What are the different types of AI?
AI can be categorized into three main types: Narrow AI, General AI, and Superintelligent AI. Narrow AI, also known as weak AI, is designed to perform specific tasks or solve particular problems. General AI aims to possess the same level of intelligence as humans and can handle various tasks across different domains. Superintelligent AI, seen in science fiction, surpasses human intelligence in almost all aspects, capable of outperforming humans in virtually any intellectual task.

4. What are some real-world applications of AI?
AI has made tremendous advancements and is now widespread in various industries. Some examples of AI applications include autonomous vehicles, virtual assistants (e.g., Siri, Alexa), recommendation systems (e.g., personalized movie recommendations), fraud detection in banking, medical diagnosis, and even predicting

stock market trends. AI's potential remains vast, and it continues to revolutionize numerous fields.

5. What are the ethical considerations surrounding AI?
As AI becomes increasingly integrated into our daily lives, ethical considerations are vital. Some concerns include the potential for job displacement due to automation, bias in AI algorithms, privacy invasion, and the impact of AI on society. It is critical to establish guidelines and regulations to ensure the responsible development and use of AI, considering both the benefits and potential risks associated with its deployment.

6. Can AI replace humans?
While AI has the potential to automate certain tasks and augment human capabilities, the idea of AI replacing humans entirely remains highly unlikely. AI excels at specific tasks, such as data analysis or pattern recognition, but it lacks the holistic understanding, creativity, and social skills that humans possess. Instead of replacing humans, AI is more likely to work alongside us, enhancing our abilities and improving efficiency.

7. How can I get started in AI research?

Embarking on a career or hobby in AI research can be both exciting and rewarding. To start, it's essential to gain a solid understanding of programming languages like Python and familiarize yourself with fundamental mathematical concepts such as linear algebra and calculus. Additionally, explore online resources, courses, and tutorials, participate in AI challenges, and join communities where you can collaborate with like-minded individuals and learn from experts in the field.

As you progress in your AI journey, remember that the field is ever-evolving, and embracing a continuous learning mindset will be invaluable. By staying informed and adapting to new developments, you can contribute to the exciting and rapidly expanding field of AI research.

## C. Recommended Resources for Advanced Learning

As you continue to delve deeper into the captivating world of Artificial Intelligence, it is important to recognize the value of continuous learning and exploration. Acquiring new knowledge, refining your skills, and staying up to date with the latest developments are essential components of your journey towards becoming an AI expert. In this section, we provide you with a carefully curated list of recommended resources that will serve as invaluable companions in your advanced learning endeavors.

1. Books:
Books have long been cherished as a fundamental source of knowledge and inspiration. Within the field of AI, there are several seminal works that have stood the test of time and are widely regarded as indispensable guides for aspiring researchers and practitioners. "Artificial Intelligence: A Modern Approach" by Stuart Russell and Peter Norvig is an excellent starting point for those seeking a comprehensive introduction to AI. Additionally, "Deep Learning" by Ian Goodfellow, Yoshua Bengio, and Aaron Courville delves into the intricacies of neural networks and their applications. For a more specialized exploration, "Pattern Recognition and Machine Learning" by Christopher Bishop provides a detailed examination of probabilistic modeling and inference in the context of AI.

2. Online Courses:
The vast realm of online education has expanded greatly in recent years, offering a multitude of AI

courses catered to individuals of all technical backgrounds. Platforms such as Coursera, edX, and Udacity host a variety of notable AI courses taught by renowned professors and industry experts. Andrew Ng's "Machine Learning" course, available on Coursera, is widely acclaimed for its insightful approach to teaching foundational AI concepts. For those specifically interested in deep learning, DeepLearning.ai's "Deep Learning Specialization" is highly recommended. Furthermore, "Fast.ai" provides a unique and practical perspective on deep learning, focusing on cutting-edge techniques and real-world applications.

3. Research Papers and Journals:
Staying abreast of the latest AI research is crucial for anyone aspiring to push the boundaries of the field. Accessing research papers and journals can offer profound insights and expose you to groundbreaking developments. Platforms like arXiv, AAAI, NeurIPS, and ICML are treasure troves of scholarly articles, providing access to a vast collection of research papers across various AI subfields. Exploring these platforms regularly will allow you to deepen your understanding of AI techniques, familiarize yourself with emerging

trends, and discover opportunities for further research and collaboration.

4. AI Conferences and Meetups:
Attending AI conferences and meetups presents extraordinary opportunities to connect with like-minded individuals, engage in thought-provoking discussions, and gain exposure to cutting-edge research. Conferences such as the Conference on Neural Information Processing Systems (NeurIPS), the International Conference on Machine Learning (ICML), and the Association for the Advancement of Artificial Intelligence (AAAI) conference are renowned events that attract leading researchers and industry experts from around the globe. Similarly, local AI meetups offer the chance to connect with practitioners in your area, exchange ideas, and potentially collaborate on exciting projects.

5. Online Communities and Forums:
Engaging with online communities and forums is an excellent way to tap into the collective intelligence of AI enthusiasts worldwide. Platforms like Reddit's r/MachineLearning and Quora's AI section serve as vibrant hubs for discussions, knowledge sharing, and seeking advice. Participating actively in these

communities enables you to learn from experienced professionals, discuss emerging concepts, and seek answers to your queries. By contributing your own insights and experiences, you can also help foster a welcoming and collaborative environment for others.

**D. GPT-4 Chat API Documentation**
Key Highlights:

1. Familiarization with GPT-4:
   - Aligned with prior chapters, we begin by taking a bird's eye view of GPT-4 and understanding its architectural modifications compared to its predecessors. Diving into its enhanced capabilities in focused dialogue-based tasks, we illuminate how GPT-4 pushes past the limitations of traditional language models. By gaining insights into the innovations of GPT-4, readers can fully comprehend and grasp the significance of these advancements.

2. Encountering the GPT-4 Commands:
   - Navigating through intricate technical specifications is made effortless as we explore the detailed API commands that enable interactive conversation turn-taking between the agent and end-users. Through comprehensible

descriptions and adapted conversational prompts, readers will ascertain the necessary skills to guide a smooth and engaging dialogue flow powered by GPT-4.

3. Fine-tuning Techniques and Instantiations:
  - Demystifying the complex terrain of fine-tuning models, we outline practical strategies that enhance GPT-4's chat functionality to better tailor it towards user-specific domains or enhance its expertise in existing problem spaces. Carefully curated methodologies give readers a comprehensive toolkit to create personalized conversational agents that align with their specific requirements.

4. Challenges, Solutions, and Ethical Considerations:
  - A wholesome understanding of artificial intelligence demands a vehement awareness of ethical implications and considerations. Engaging readers in critical reflections, we provide effective measures to tackle challenges such as biases and misinformation while designing conversation agents. Deepening consciousness regarding ethics invites a responsible and trustworthy approach to AI development.

www.ingramcontent.com/pod-product-compliance
Lightning Source LLC
La Vergne TN
LVHW051345050326
832903LV00031B/3745